HOMEMADE DESSERTS

HOMEMADE DESSERTS

Maggie Mayhew
Catherine Atkinson
Caroline Barty

Photography by Ian Garlick

MQP

An Hachette Livre UK Company
First published in Great Britain in 2006 by MQ Publications,
a division of Octopus Publishing Group Ltd
2–4 Heron Quays
London E14 4JP

www.octopusbooks.co.uk

Copyright © Octopus Publishing Group Ltd 2006, 2008
Recipes: Catherine Atkinson, Caroline Barty, Maggie Mayhew
Photography: Ian Garlick
Home Economy: Alice Hart
Illustrations: Penny Brown

ISBN 978-1-84601-139-9

Printed and bound in China

10 9 8 7 6 5 4 3 2

IMPORTANT: Those who might be at risk from the effects of salmonella
poisoning (the elderly, pregnant women, young children and
those suffering from immune deficiency diseases) should consult
their GP with any concerns about eating raw eggs.

Contents

Introduction

There is always room for a bit of dessert. Whether it is your grannie's secret recipe apple pie, a naughty chocolate treat shared with a friend, or the amazing concoction presented by your host at a dinner party, everyone loves a homemade dish. As we were growing up, many of our mums and grandmothers wouldn't have dreamed of buying a pre-packaged dessert to round off a meal. Now that mass-market brands have made this type of ready-made food available, and since many more of us work full-time, we seem to have hung up our aprons for good. We see a layered cake or a colourful trifle at the supermarket and think we could never make it ourselves. But baking a pie or whipping up a fruity mousse can be one of the most enjoyable ends to a day in the office, and it's something the whole family can get involved with – and enjoy the results.

Split into six chapters – Grandma's Best, Chocolate Heaven, Cool and Creamy, Pies and Tarts, Fruity Favourites, and Dinner Party Delights – *Homemade Desserts* guides you through each recipe step-by-step, providing helpful tips on preparation techniques, serving suggestions, and storage advice along the way. A comprehensive introduction takes you through the basics, providing you with the skills needed to produce stunning desserts, from beautifully turned out pastry to deliciously smooth ice cream. Start out simple with recipes like Fried Bananas with Rum and Brown Sugar or Spiced Baked Apples, and as you gain confidence try your hand at more complicated recipes like Freeform Strawberry Rhubarb Pie and Pavlova with Tropical Fruits. Making your own food is the best way to control what you eat, and *Homemade Desserts* shows you how to make the most out of fresh and wholesome ingredients.

The recipes that follow will win back your enthusiasm for the kitchen, as well as encourage all the family to eat well and to eat together. Every recipe is an achievable goal, so rise to the challenge, and wow your next group of dinner guests with a scrumptious soufflé, tower of profiteroles, or fruity meringue. If you haven't baked since you were at school, start with easy recipes and try to make something different once a week. After a few months everyone will have a favourite, and you will be inundated with requests. Don't worry if your first few attempts look a bit wonky – that's the beauty of a homemade dessert, even the raw ingredients taste good. Remember licking the spoon when you were growing up? Enjoying your mistakes is all part of the learning curve. As your confidence grows you will find yourself swapping pastry tips, and have found a few of your own secret ingredients.

Dessert Techniques & Tips

THE BASICS

Whipping cream

It is important to start with chilled cream – either double or whipping cream – and use a cold bowl, preferably ceramic, stainless steel or glass. The best style of whisk to use is a balloon, hand-held electric or old-fashioned hand-held rotary whisk. Whip quickly to begin with until the cream starts to thicken and becomes the consistency of custard.

Now's the time to reduce the whipping speed so you don't over whip. If you continue whipping for a short while, the cream will begin to hold its shape but will drop easily from a spoon. At this stage it is of spooning consistency. It will have some texture but won't hold its shape for long.

If you whip for a few seconds more, the cream should start to hold its shape and will have a glossy sheen. Once you get to this stage, the cream is perfect for serving, as it will thicken slightly on standing or piping.

Make sure you don't over whip your cream. If you keep whipping past this stage, the cream will form stiff peaks and become too thick and buttery in texture. If over-whipped cream is left at room temperature it may even separate out into curds and whey.

Whisking egg whites

Whisking is a vital process in the making of a meringue. When egg whites are whisked, they increase their volume and become frothy, light and airy. They will achieve a better volume if they are left at room temperature for a couple of hours, and not used cold, straight from the refrigerator.

Use a balloon or egg whisk for the best volume and texture, but if you are not used to whisking by hand, or speed is of the essence, an electric hand-held or tabletop whisk will be fine. Separate the eggs, allowing the whites to drop into a grease-free, non-reactive bowl. If any egg yolk falls in with it, remove before starting to whisk. The easiest way to do this is to use one of the broken eggshells: for some quirky reason the yolk is attracted to the shell. Whisk quickly and lightly in an even, steady movement. The egg whites will become frothy but still liquid.

If you continue whisking past this stage the egg whites will become stiff but smooth. This is the stiff peak stage, when sugar or syrup can be added. A good way to check if this stage has been reached is to tip the bowl. If the egg whites begin to slide out of the bowl they need further whisking.

If sugar is to be added, lightly sprinkle it over the top, a spoonful at a time, whisking well in between each addition. When the egg whites are very stiff and glossy the remaining sugar or ingredients can be folded in gently with a metal spoon to prevent knocking out the air.

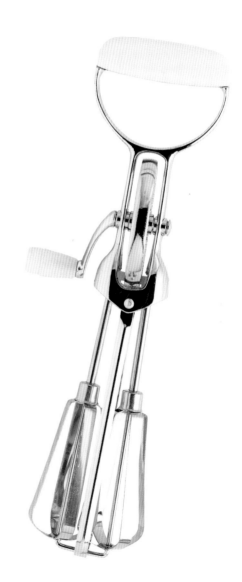

TIPS FOR SUCCESSFUL PIE MAKING

Equipment

Using the correct baking equipment simplifies and enhances pie making, but few specialist implements are essential. You probably already possess the basic items: standard measuring cups and spoons or accurate weighing scales, a calibrated pitcher, a good-sized mixing bowl, a fine strainer, and a few sharp knives. Other important items include:

ROLLING PIN
A thick, heavy one is best for rolling out pastry, although marble rolling pins are cooler.

TIMER
Vital when pie making.

PIE PLATES AND DISHES
In glass or porcelain, which have an unglazed base to allow heat to penetrate. These are especially useful for single-crust pies.

TART PANS
The best are metal with fluted sides, which are easier to line. Loose bases will simplify removal.

PASTRY BRUSH
For even glazing.

BAKING BEANS
For 'baking blind'. Choose ceramic or aluminium ones, which last forever and are food heat conductors, or simply use dried beans or pulses.

WIRE RACK
To allow air to circulate and prevent sogginess when cooling pie shells.

PIE PANS AND DISHES
When deciding on which pan to use it is best to be led by the recipe. For an open pie or tart, recipes usually call for a metal loose-bottomed tart pan. These are generally favoured above china ones because they conduct heat more efficiently – the last thing you want is soggy, undercooked pastry! Loose-bottomed pans also allow the pie to be transferred easily onto a serving plate, which makes it a lot easier to cut slices. It's also worth investing in good old-fashioned shallow and deep pie dishes. The gentle sloping sides make lining the dishes easy and the pastry won't slip down if you're blind baking. Finally remember that if you change the dish size from the recipe you will have to adjust the cooking times: a smaller, deeper pie will take longer to cook than a shallow, wide one.

Ingredients

Most pastry doughs are created from three simple ingredients: flour, shortening, and water. Used in the correct proportions and handled correctly, these make delicious, flaky pie crusts. The addition of egg or egg yolk, sweetener, and flavouring are ways of altering the taste and texture of the final product.

Traditional pastry calls for plain flour, and no other type should be used unless specified in the recipe. Self-raising flour produces softer pastry and may be used in a suet-crust. Wholemeal makes a much heavier dough, but it is sometimes used together with plain flour. Pastry can be made with one fat or a mixture. Butter on its own gives an excellent flavour and colour. If margarine is preferred it should be the hard-block variety. White vegetable fat, or shortening, makes shorter, more flaky pastry and is often used with butter in equal amounts.

Making perfect pastry

There are many different types of pastry, from buttery, layered puff, and flaky pastry to paper-thin filo, also known as strudel pastry. Shortcrust is probably the best known and most frequently used for pie making. While it's the simplest of all pastries, it needs a cool, light hand and you should avoid overhandling the dough or it will become tough.

PASTRY METHODS
MANUAL VS. FOOD PROCESSOR
Throughout this book you will find different

methods for making pastry. Some require the rubbing-in method, others tell you to use the food processor, If you don't like getting your hands dirty you can use the food processor all the time but, to my mind, the best, lightest pastry is made by the hands-on method. The main thing to remember is to keep the butter and water cold and not to overwork the dough. Go easy when adding the water – too much and you will end up with tough pastry. You can tell how much water to add by feeling the texture of the dough.

Shortcrust pastry: the basic method

There is a great deal of mystique surrounding the making of shortcrust pastry. In fact, the method is very straightforward and just takes a little practice. If you're worried that your hands are too warm to rub the butter in as described below, try using two knives to cut the butter into small pieces. Rest the dough before rolling or it may shrink on cooking, producing an uneven result.

To make enough shortcrust pastry to line a 23cm flan tin, you'll need 175g plain flour, a pinch salt, 85g cold butter, diced, and 2-3 tablespoons cold water.

STEP 1

Sift the flour into a mixing bowl with the salt. Add the butter and using your fingertips, rub or cut the butter into the flour until the mixture resembles coarse breadcrumbs.

STEP 2

Add 2 tablespoons of the water and using your hands, start to bring the dough together, adding a little more water if necessary. Do not use too much water or the resulting pastry will be tough.

STEP 3

Turn the dough onto a lightly floured surface and knead briefly, just until the dough is smooth. Form into a neat ball, flatten into a disc, and wrap in cling film. Chill at least 30 minutes.

STEP 4

Remove the pastry from the fridge. Unwrap and put onto a lightly floured surface. Lightly flour the top of the dough under the rolling pin while rolling it back and forth. Try not to stretch the dough by pulling - allow the weight and pressure of the pin to roll the dough.

STEP 5

Roll the pastry into a rough circle at least 5cm in diameter larger than a loose-bottomed 23cm fluted flan tin. Gently roll the pastry onto the rolling pin, and then unroll it over the tin to cover. Carefully press the pastry into the edge of the tin, removing any overhanging pastry with a knife.

STEP 6

Prick the base all over with a fork, being careful not to make holes right through the dough. This helps to keep the dough from rising in the middle during baking. Chill 20 minutes.

6 steps to shortcrust success

1 Always sift flour to remove lumps and incorporate air.

2 When making pastry, use fat that is cool but not hard.

3 Always chill shortcrust before rolling, and before baking. This allows the gluten to 'relax,' preventing shrinkage.

4 After chilling pastry, leave at room temperature for a few minutes before rolling out.

5 Roll pastry in short, gentle strokes, lightly and evenly in one direction only. Keep turning it to stop it sticking.

6 If you need a large amount of pastry (if making several pies), make it in batches.

Rough puff pastry: the basic method

This is an unusual method for making rough puff pastry, as the dough includes baking powder and is bound with buttermilk. This helps to give the pastry a good rise as well as an excellent flavour. It produces a dough that is softer than butter puff pastry and so is best suited to savoury rather than sweet recipes. This dough can be frozen, well wrapped, for up to 2 months. Allow to thaw completely before using. See the recipe on page 14 to prepare the basic rough dough pastry.

1 Sift the flour, salt, baking powder and bicarbonate of soda into a mixing bowl. Cut the butter into dice, add to the flour, and rub together, using your fingertips until the mixture resembles very coarse breadcrumbs. The pieces of butter should still be discernible, but all coated in flour.

2 Follow steps 1, 2 and 3 (see page 14).

3 Transfer the dough to a baking sheet or tray lined with baking parchment. Cover with cling film and chill, about 20 minutes.

4 Remove from the refrigerator and repeat the rolling and folding twice more. Prepare to this point if using to top a pie or for use in the recipe that follows.

STEP 1

Stir in about half the buttermilk and begin mixing the dough together, adding just enough of the remaining buttermilk to make a soft dough.

STEP 2

Turn the dough onto a floured surface and dust with flour as well. Roll the dough out to 2cm thick. Lift the dough from the surface and fold it, like a letter, in thirds.

STEP 3

Give the dough a quarter turn. Flour the surface and dough again and reroll the dough into a rectangle, of the same thickness. Repeat the folding and turning.

Rolling out technique

This is often the part that puts people off making their own pastry. The first thing to remember is to rest the dough – nine times out of ten if someone is having trouble rolling out pastry it is because they skipped the resting period. Resting is essential as the gluten in the flour reacts with liquid and becomes elastic and pliable over time. This will make the pastry easier to roll out and less liable to tear or crumble. Wrap the pastry in cling film and leave in the fridge for at least 20 minutes. When you take it out of the fridge allow it to rest at room temperature for 5 to 10 minutes to soften a little. Shape the dough with your hands into the shape of the tin you are using. So if you are using a rectangular tin roughly shape the dough into a rectangle – this just makes it easier to roll out into the right proportions. Don't turn the pastry during rolling – there is a chance it will tear and shrink too much.

Lining a tart pan

1 On a lightly floured surface, roll out the pastry to a thickness of ⅛in/3mm and to a circle about 2 to 3in/5 to 7.5cm larger than the tart tin, depending on the depth of the tin.

2 Lift the pastry with the rolling pin and ease it into the tin. Press the pastry against the side of the tin so that there are no gaps. Roll the rolling pin over the top of the tin to cut off the excess dough.

3 Prick the base of the dough liberally, and then chill for at least 10 minutes, to prevent puffing and shrinkage during baking.

Baking blind

This is used either to partly cook an empty pie shell, so that is does not become soggy when the filling is added, or to completely bake a pie shell when the filling isn't baked.

1 To bake the pie shell partially, cover the pastry with baking parchment or foil and fill with dried or baking beans. Bake at 200°C/400°F/Gas mark 6 for 10 to 15 minutes. Remove the paper or foil and beans. Brush with beaten egg, if the filling is moist, to seal the base. Bake for 5 minutes more.

2 To fully bake the pie shell, follow the above, but bake for 10 minutes after the paper or foil are removed, or until golden brown. Cool before filling.

Keeping and freezing pastry

Uncooked puff, shortcrust, and most other pastries can be stored chilled for several days in cling film to prevent them from drying out. Pastry may also be frozen for several weeks; thaw in the refrigerator overnight, then leave at room temperature for 15 minutes before rolling out. You can also freeze sheets of rolled out pastry, placed on baking parchment on a baking tray and covered with cling film. Unbaked pie shells will keep covered in the refrigerator for 2 to 3 days, or for a week in the freezer. Fully baked pie shells may be frozen or kept in an airtight container for a day or two.

Baking tips

- Always bake pie shells and double-crust pies on a heated baking tray. This helps to crispen the pastry base and also catch any drips should the filled shell or pie bubble over.
- If you find any small holes in a cooked pie shell, repair them by brushing with beaten egg, then return to the oven for 2 to 3 minutes to seal.
- If the pastry has fully browned before the filling is cooked, protect it with foil. Cover single and double-crust pies completely, making a hole in the foil to let steam escape. On open pie shells, cover the pastry edge only with strips of foil.

TIPS FOR SUCCESSFUL ICE CREAM AND FROZEN DESSERTS

Below are some tips and tricks to perfect frozen desserts.

- Ice cream is best when stored between –21°C/ -5°F and -18°C/0°F.

- Never let ice cream melt and refreeze. It won't look too appetising.

- The faster the ice cream freezes, the smoother the texture.

- Create mixtures for churn-frozen ice creams the day before you freeze, to increase yield and produce a smoother texture.

- Make sure ice cream is covered so that it does not absorb flavours from other foods.

- As a rule, fill the churn/machine no more than two-thirds full to allow room for expansion.

- Allow 5 to 6 litres of chipped or cracked ice to 250g of coarse rock salt for old-fashioned machines, and let the ice stand for 3 minutes before beginning.

- For hand-crank machines, begin with a slow crank, about 40 turns per minute until you feel the mixture begin to thicken by resistance. Then triple your speed for 5–6 minutes. Add any chopped fruit after this step before repacking the salt ice and finishing with about 80 turns per minute for another few minutes to finish.

- Overfilling the inner container with the ice cream mixture, too much salt in the ice-packing mixture, and/or churning too rapidly can result in a granular texture.

- For ices, use no more than 1 part sugar to 4 parts liquid. The ice will not freeze properly if there is too much sugar. The larger the proportion of sugar or other sweetener, the slower the mixture freezes. Any alcohol should be added after the ice has frozen.

- Whipped cream or evaporated milk, melted marshmallows, beaten eggs, gelatine and other ingredients are all additives used to prevent the formation of large ice crystals as well as improve or vary flavour. A tip to avoid ice crystals: add 1 envelope of unflavoured gelatine per 6 cups of ice cream mixture. Let the gelatine soften in $\frac{1}{4}$ cup of the mixture, then gently heat it until it is dissolved. Add to the remaining mixture and proceed.

- After your ice cream is done, let it sit in the freezer for four hours before eating it to let it develop flavour and texture.

Ice cream: the basic method

An ice cream base is made by combining a custard mixture with whipped cream. It's frozen for short bursts and whisked to break down the ice crystals formed during freezing. To make about 450ml of vanilla ice cream, you will need 150ml full fat milk, ½ vanilla pod, 2 egg yolks, 4 tablespoons caster sugar and 300ml double cream.

STEP 1

Bring the milk and vanilla pod to simmering point over low heat. Remove the pan from the heat then remove the vanilla pod. Whisk the egg yolks and sugar with a hand-held electric whisk until pale and slightly thickened. Lightly whisk in the hot milk.

STEP 2

Pour into a heavy-based pan. Cook over a low heat, stirring constantly until the mixture thickens to the consistency of double cream and coats the back of the spoon.

STEP 3

Tear off some cling film and then press down over the surface of the custard (this will stop a skin from forming) and set to one side to go cold.

STEP 4

Pour the cream into a bowl. Using a hand-held electric whisk, whip the cream until it forms stiff peaks. When the custard is cold, fold in the cream.

STEP 5

Pour into a freezer container and freeze until half-frozen. Whisk to break up the ice crystals then return to the freezer. Repeat twice more until thick. Stir in the flavourings and, finally freeze until firm. Alternatively, churn in an ice cream maker.

GRANDMA'S BEST

- Pumpkin Pie
- Shoofly Pie
- Sweet Raisin Pie
- Four Berry Pie
- Fruity Bread & Butter Pudding
- Sticky Toffee Pudding
- Blackcurrant Pie
- Peach & Raspberry Pies
- Peach Cake
- Sweet Potato Pie
- Eggnog Tart
- Apple Strudel
- Sweet Vanilla Soufflé
- Black Cherry & Chocolate Cake
- Cherry Cinnamon Cobbler
- Grape Pie
- Deep-Dish Apple Pie à la Mode
- Banoffee Pie
- Two-Crust Prune Pie
- Peach Cobbler
- Cranberry Pie
- Key Lime Pie
- Blackberry & Apple Pie
- Cherry Strudel
- Linzertorte with a Lattice Top
- Hot Waffles & Banana with Toffee Brandy Sauce
- Swiss Roll with Lemon Cream
- Crumb Pie
- Baked Apples with Walnut Jackets
- Banana & Toffee Cheesecake

CHAPTER ONE

GRANDMA'S BEST

Pumpkin Pie

Serves 6–8

350g plain flour, plus extra for dusting
Pinch of salt
175g butter
4–5 tablespoons water
Single cream, to serve

For the filling

900g pumpkin to yield 675g pumpkin
  pulp, flesh cut into 5cm pieces
2 eggs, beaten
90g brown sugar
240ml golden syrup
240ml double cream
2 teaspoons ground cinnamon
1 teaspoon ground ginger
½ teaspoon freshly grated nutmeg
1 teaspoon vanilla extract

1 Sift the flour and salt into a mixing bowl. Add the butter and rub it in until the mixture resembles breadcrumbs. Add 4 tablespoons cold water and mix to a firm dough, adding more water, if necessary. Knead until smooth. Wrap in cling film and chill for 20 minutes.

2 Roll out the pastry on a lightly floured surface into a rough round at least 5cm larger than a loose-bottomed 30cm fluted tart tin. Line the tin and trim off any excess pastry. Prick the base all over. Chill for 20 minutes. Put a baking tray in the oven and preheat to 200°C/400°F/Gas mark 6.

3 Line the pastry case with greaseproof paper and fill with baking beans. Bake for 20 minutes. Remove the paper and beans. Reduce the oven temperature to 190°C/375°F/Gas mark 5. Put the pumpkin in a saucepan and cover with water. Bring to the boil, then simmer for 15 minutes, or until tender. Drain the pumpkin, cool and purée, then spoon into a large bowl.

4 Add the eggs, sugar, golden syrup and double cream to the pumpkin purée and mix. Stir in the spices and vanilla extract. Spoon the mixture into the pastry case and bake for 30-35 minutes, or until set. Serve warm with cream.

Shoofly Pie

Serves 6–8

175g plain flour, plus extra for dusting
Pinch of salt
90g butter, diced
About 2 tablespoons cold water
Custard or cream, to serve

For the filling
2 eggs, lightly beaten
115g plain flour
115g dark brown sugar
¼ teaspoon each ground ginger and
   nutmeg
½ teaspoon ground cinnamon
75g butter, diced
185g molasses
100ml boiling water
½ teaspoon bicarbonate of soda

1 Sift the flour and salt into a mixing bowl. Add the butter and rub it in until the mixture resembles fine breadcrumbs. Sprinkle the water over the flour mixture, and stir together to make a firm dough. Knead briefly, then form the dough into a neat ball, wrap in cling film and chill for 30 minutes. Meanwhile, put a baking tray in the oven and preheat to 200°C/400°F/Gas mark 6.

2 Roll out the pastry on a lightly floured surface and use to line a 23cm pie dish. Trim and flute the edges, then prick the base all over with a fork. Chill for 15 minutes.

3 Line the pastry case with greaseproof paper and fill with baking beans. Bake blind for 15 minutes. Remove the paper and beans, brush the base with 1 teaspoon beaten egg from the filling, and bake for 5 minutes. Remove from the oven and reduce the temperature to 190°C/375°F/Gas mark 5.

4 For the filling, sift the flour into a bowl. Stir in the brown sugar and spices. Rub in the butter until the mixture resembles coarse breadcrumbs. Sprinkle a third over the base of the pastry case.

5 Beat the eggs and molasses together in a bowl. Pour the boiling water into a large jug and stir in the bicarbonate of soda (it will froth up, so make sure there's room for this). Immediately pour into the egg mixture and beat together.

6 Quickly pour the mixture into the pastry case and sprinkle evenly with the remaining spice mixture. Bake for 30–35 minutes, or until firm and browned. Serve warm or at room temperature with custard or cream. For a Kentucky pie, leave out the spices and add more dried fruit.

Sweet Raisin Pie

Serves 8–10

175g plain flour, plus extra for dusting
115g unsalted butter, diced
2 teaspoons sugar
1 egg, lightly beaten

For the filling
115g unsalted butter
225g light brown sugar
1 teaspoon ground cinnamon
½ teaspoon ground allspice
Pinch of freshly grated nutmeg
4 egg yolks
2 tablespoons plain flour
240ml double cream
75g raisins
75g chopped dates
75g chopped pecan nuts

1 Sift the flour into a bowl. Add the butter and rub it in until the mixture resembles breadcrumbs. Stir in the sugar, add all but 2 teaspoons of the beaten egg and mix to a firm dough. Knead briefly, then form into a neat ball, wrap in cling film and chill for 30 minutes.

2 Put a baking tray in the oven and preheat to 200°C/400°F/Gas mark 6. Roll out the pastry on a lightly floured surface and use to line a shallow 23cm tart tin. Prick the base all over with a fork then chill for 10 minutes.

3 Line the pastry case with greaseproof paper and fill with baking beans. Bake blind for 15 minutes. Remove the paper and beans and bake for 5 minutes. Reduce the oven temperature to 160°C/325°F/Gas mark 3.

4 For the filling, cream the butter, sugar and spices together in a bowl until light then beat in the egg yolks, one at a time. Sift over the flour and beat in, then stir in the double cream, raisins, dates and nuts.

5 Spoon the filling into the pastry case and bake for 30 minutes, or until lightly set. Leave to settle for 10 minutes, then serve warm.

Four Berry Pie

Serves 6

300g plain flour, plus extra for dusting
1 tablespoon sugar
1 teaspoon grated orange zest
175g butter, diced
2½–3 tablespoons cold water
Whipped cream, to serve

For the filling
250g raspberries
175g blackberries
115g blueberries
115g hulled strawberries, quartered
50g sugar, or to taste
1 tablespoon cornflour
Beaten egg, for glazing
1 tablespoon icing sugar

1 Sift the flour and sugar into a mixing bowl, then stir in the orange zest. Add the butter and rub it in until the mixture resembles fine breadcrumbs. Sprinkle over 2½ tablespoons of the water and mix to a firm dough, adding the remaining water if needed. Wrap in cling film and chill for 30 minutes.

2 To make the filling, put the fruit into a bowl with the quartered strawberries at the top, then sprinkle over the sugar. After a few minutes, gently toss the fruit with your hands to coat it in the sugar. Leave for 20 minutes. Meanwhile, put a baking tray in the oven and preheat to 200°C/400°F/Gas mark 6.

3 Roll out about two-thirds of the pastry on a lightly floured surface to a round about 4cm larger all round than a shallow 20–23cm pie dish. Line the pie dish, leaving an overhang of pastry, and then dampen the edge with a little water.

4 Carefully transfer the fruit to the pastry case using your hands. Blend the cornflour and the fruit juice at the bottom of the bowl together to form a smooth paste, and drizzle this over the fruit.

5 Roll out the remaining pastry to make a lid and use to cover the pie, pressing the edges together well to seal. Trim the excess pastry with a knife. Crimp the edge of the pie and make decorations from the re-rolled pastry trimmings.

6 Brush the pie with beaten egg to glaze, then sprinkle over the icing sugar. Slash the top twice or make small holes with a skewer to allow steam to escape. Bake for 35–45 minutes, or until the pastry is a deep golden brown. Let the pie settle for 10 minutes before serving with whipped cream.

Fruity Bread & Butter Pudding

Serves 8

75g unsalted butter, softened, plus
   extra for greasing
300ml milk
300ml double cream
1 vanilla pod, split
About 6 slices day-old white bread,
   crusts removed
2 tablespoons apricot jam
2 tablespoons dried apricots, chopped
1 tablespoon raisins
2 tablespoons sultanas
6 egg yolks
4 tablespoons sugar
Single cream, to serve

Tip

Make a number of delicious versions by substituting the white loaf with croissants, brioche, panettone or French bread.

1 Preheat the oven to 180°C/350°F/Gas mark 4. Lightly grease a shallow 1.2 litre ovenproof dish.

2 Put the milk, cream and vanilla pod into a saucepan and heat gently until simmering. Remove from heat and leave to infuse for 15 minutes.

3 Butter the bread generously. Spread half the slices with the apricot jam. Cut each slice into 4 triangles and use the bread spread with jam to line the base of the dish. Scatter the apricots, raisins and sultanas over the bread in the dish. Arrange the remaining bread triangles attractively on top.

4 Meanwhile, whisk the egg yolks and sugar together until pale and creamy. Strain the milk and cream mixture on to the egg yolks and sugar, whisking all the time. Carefully pour the custard mixture over the bread as evenly as possible. Press the bread gently into the custard. Set aside for 20-30 minutes.

5 Transfer the dish to the oven and bake for 30-35 minutes until the custard is just set and the bread is golden and crisp on top. Serve warm with cream.

Sticky Toffee Pudding

Serves 2

50g butter, softened, plus extra for
   greasing
50g brown sugar
1 egg, beaten
100g self-raising flour
55g chopped dates
2 tablespoons milk

For the sauce
75g brown sugar
125ml double cream
50g butter

1 Grease a 1 litre pudding basin. Beat the butter and sugar together in a separate bowl until light and fluffy, then beat in the egg a little at a time. Fold in the flour, then stir in the dates and enough of the milk to give the mixture a soft, dropping consistency.

2 Spoon the mixture into the prepared pudding basin. Cut a round of greaseproof paper and a round of foil about 5cm larger than the top of the basin, and grease the bottom of the paper. Place both over the bowl and secure with string.

3 Put the bowl in a large saucepan and pour boiling water around the bowl, to come two-thirds of the way up the sides. Cover and simmer for 1–1½ hours until risen and springy when pressed. Check the water occasionally, topping up if necessary.

4 Put all the sauce ingredients in a small saucepan and heat gently, stirring, until combined. Simmer for 5 minutes, or until thickened. Turn the pudding out on to a plate and serve with the sauce.

Blackcurrant Pie

Serves 6

75g plain flour, plus extra for dusting
50g wholemeal flour
Pinch of salt
65g chilled butter, diced
1 teaspoon grated orange zest
2 tablespoons cold water
Beaten egg, for glazing
1 tablespoon demerara sugar, for
   sprinkling
Custard or cream, to serve

For the filling
800g blackcurrants
75g sugar, or to taste
2 tablespoons cornflour, sifted
Juice of ½ small orange
15g butter

1 Sift the flours and salt into a bowl. Add the bran left in the sieve, then add the butter and rub it in until the mixture resembles breadcrumbs. Stir in the orange zest, then sprinkle the water over the dry ingredients and mix to a firm dough. Knead briefly, wrap in cling film and chill for 30 minutes.

2 Tip the blackcurrants into a large bowl. Mix the sugar and cornflour together and sprinkle over the blackcurrants. Squeeze over the orange juice, then toss together. Leave to stand for 10 minutes.

3 Preheat the oven to 200°C/400°F/Gas mark 6. Using an inverted 23cm pie dish as a guide, roll out the pastry on a floured surface until it is 5cm larger all round than the dish. Cut a 2.5cm strip from around the edge. Moisten the rim of the dish and position the strip on the rim. Brush with water.

4 Spoon the filling into the dish, mounding it in the centre. Dot the top with butter. Place the pastry lid on top, seal and crimp the edges, and snip a hole in the top to allow steam to escape. Brush with beaten egg and sprinkle with demerara sugar.

5 Bake for 20 minutes, then reduce the temperature to 180°C/350°F/Gas mark 4 and bake for 15-25 minutes, or until the pastry is lightly browned and crisp. Serve with custard or cream.

Peach & Raspberry Pies

Serves 4

225g plain flour, plus extra for dusting
Pinch of salt
115g butter, diced
3–4 tablespoons cold water

For the filling
4 large ripe peaches, stoned and
    roughly chopped
115g raspberries
75g caster sugar, plus extra for
    sprinkling
Juice of ½ lemon
1 tablespoon milk, for glazing
Crème fraîche or soured cream,
    to serve

1 Sift the flour and salt into a mixing bowl. Add the butter and rub it in until the mixture resembles coarse breadcrumbs. Add 2 tablespoons water and using your hands, start to bring the dough together, adding a little more water if necessary. Knead, then form the dough into a neat ball, wrap in cling film and chill for 30 minutes.

2 Mix the peaches, raspberries, sugar and lemon juice together in a bowl and set aside.

3 Preheat the oven to 200°C/400°F/Gas mark 6. Divide the pastry into 4 equal portions. Working with one portion at a time, divide into one-third and two-thirds. Roll out the larger piece to fit a 10cm round pie tin. Add a quarter of the peach mixture. Wet the edges of the pastry and roll out the smaller portion of pastry. Use to top the pie, trimming off the excess and crimping the edges to seal. Snip a hole in the top of the pie to allow steam to escape.

4 Brush the pastry with a little milk and sprinkle with caster sugar. Repeat to make 4 pies. Transfer the pies to the oven and bake for about 20–25 minutes, or until the pastry is golden.

5 Leave to cool for about 10 minutes, then carefully turn the pies out of their tins. Serve with crème fraîche or soured cream.

Peach Cake

Makes 10–12 slices

175g unsalted butter, softened
175g caster sugar
3 eggs, beaten
200g ground almonds
100g self-raising flour
2 teaspoons vanilla extract
425g can peach halves in fruit juice,
  drained
Sifted icing sugar, to dust

1 Preheat the oven to 180°C/350°F/Gas mark 4. Grease and base line a deep 23cm round cake tin.

2 Cream the butter and caster sugar together in a bowl until pale and fluffy, then gradually add the eggs, beating well after each addition. Stir in the ground almonds, flour and vanilla extract.

3 Spoon the mixture into the prepared tin and level the surface. Arrange the peach halves, cut-side down, over the top.

4 Bake in the oven for 35–40 minutes, or until risen and golden. Cool in the tin for 10 minutes, then turn out onto a wire rack, invert the cake so that the peaches are on top and leave to cool completely. Dust with the sifted icing sugar. Serve in slices.

Sweet Potato Pie

Serves 6–8

175g plain flour, plus extra for dusting
Pinch of salt
90g chilled butter, diced
2 tablespoons cold water
Cream, to serve

For the filling
700g sweet potatoes, peeled and cut
  into large chunks
240ml single cream
2 eggs, lightly beaten
50g butter, softened
50g light brown sugar
½ teaspoon ground cinnamon
½ teaspoon ground ginger
¼ teaspoon freshly grated nutmeg
1 teaspoon vanilla extract

1 Sift the flour and salt into a bowl. Add the butter and rub it in until the mixture resembles fine breadcrumbs. Sprinkle over the water and mix to a dough. Knead, then wrap and chill for 30 minutes.

2 Put a baking tray in the oven and preheat to 200°C/400°F/Gas mark 6. Roll out the pastry on a floured surface and use to line a 23cm tart tin. Prick the base all over then chill for 10 minutes.

3 Put the sweet potatoes in a non-stick roasting tin, cover with foil and roast for 30 minutes, or until soft. Remove, and while warm, mash them in a bowl until very smooth with a few spoonfuls of the cream. About halfway through the potatoes' cooking time, line the pastry case with non-stick baking paper and fill with baking beans. Bake for 15 minutes, remove the paper and beans, brush with 1 teaspoon beaten egg from the filling and bake for a further 5 minutes. Reduce the temperature to 180°C/350°F/Gas mark 4.

4 Cream the butter and sugar together in a bowl until light. Gradually beat in the eggs, then stir in the spices and vanilla. Stir the remaining cream into the mashed sweet potato until mixed. Spoon into the pastry case. Bake for 40–45 minutes, or until lightly browned. Serve with cream.

Eggnog Tart

Serves 6–8

250g plain flour, plus extra for dusting
Pinch of salt
75g cold unsalted butter, diced
55g white vegetable fat
2–3 tablespoons cold water

For the filling
4 eggs, separated
115g granulated sugar
250ml Advocaat liqueur
300ml single cream
4 tablespoons boiling water
10g powdered gelatine
Soft fruit, such as blackberries,
   raspberries or strawberries,
   to decorate (optional)

1 Sift the flour and salt into a mixing bowl. Add the fat and rub it in until the mixture resembles coarse breadcrumbs. Add 2 tablespoons water and using your hands, bring the dough together, adding a little more water if necessary. Knead briefly, then wrap in cling film and chill for 30 minutes.

2 Roll out the pastry on a lightly floured surface and use to line a loose-bottomed 23cm tart tin. Prick the pastry with a fork and chill for 10 minutes.

3 Preheat the oven to 190°C/375°F/Gas mark 5. Line the pastry case with greaseproof paper and fill with baking beans. Bake blind for 20 minutes. Remove the paper and beans and cook for a further 5 minutes. Leave to cool completely.

4 For the filling, beat the egg yolks, sugar and liqueur together in a bowl. Bring the cream to the boil in a non-stick saucepan. Pour the cream over the egg yolks and mix well. Return to the pan and stir over a low heat until the sauce thickens enough to coat the back of a spoon. Remove from the heat.

5 Pour the boiling water into a small bowl. Sprinkle over the gelatine and stir well until dissolved. Pour into the custard mixture and mix well. Leave the custard to cool, then chill until thickened and on the point of setting.

6 Whisk the egg whites in a clean, grease-free bowl until stiff peaks form, then fold into the custard. Pour the mixture into the pastry case and level out. Chill for a further 30 minutes then decorate with soft fruit.

Apple Strudel

Serves 8

6 large sheets of filo pastry, about
   55g, thawed if frozen
50g butter, melted, plus extra for
   greasing
2 tablespoons icing sugar, for dusting
Soured cream or crème fraîche,
   to serve

For the filling
650g (about 7) eating apples
75g raisins
Grated zest and juice of ½ lemon
25g fresh white breadcrumbs
3 tablespoons granulated sugar
½ teaspoon ground cinnamon

1 Remove the filo pastry from the refrigerator and leave, still in its wrapping, at room temperature for 20 minutes.

2 Meanwhile, peel, core and thinly slice the apples. Put them in a bowl with the raisins and lemon zest. Sprinkle with the lemon juice and toss to coat. Add the breadcrumbs, sugar and cinnamon, and mix again.

3 Preheat the oven to 190°C/375°F/Gas mark 5 and grease a large baking tray. Lay one sheet of filo pastry on a damp tea towel, and lightly brush with melted butter. Place a second sheet on top. Continue to layer the filo, brushing butter between each sheet.

4 Spoon the apple mixture over the filo pastry leaving a 2.5cm margin around the edges. Turn in the short pastry edges. With the help of the tea towel, roll up from a long edge to completely enclose the filling.

5 Transfer the strudel to the prepared baking tray, seam-side down. Brush with butter and bake for 35–40 minutes until the apples are soft. If necessary, cover the pastry loosely with foil to prevent overbrowning. Dust with icing sugar and serve hot with soured cream or crème fraîche.

Sweet Vanilla Soufflé

Serves 6

300ml milk
1 vanilla pod, split
100g caster sugar
50g butter, plus extra for greasing
50g plain flour
Granulated sugar, for sprinkling
3 large eggs, separated
1 egg white
Icing sugar, for dusting

1 Put the milk, vanilla pod and caster sugar in a medium saucepan and bring to the boil over a low heat, then set aside to cool.

2 Scrape the vanilla seeds out of the pod with the point of a sharp knife, and add to the milk. Discard the pod. Melt the butter in a small saucepan and stir in the flour. Cook for 1 minute. Remove from the heat and gradually whisk in the milk. Return the pan to the heat and bring to the boil, stirring all the time.

3 Cook for 1 minute, then remove from the heat and cover the surface of the sauce with cling film. Set aside to cool slightly.

4 Preheat the oven to 190°C/375°F/Gas mark 5. Liberally grease six 175ml soufflé dishes and sprinkle the insides with sugar. Whisk the egg yolks into the cooled sauce until smooth. Whisk the egg whites in a clean, grease-free bowl until stiff peaks form. Spoon half into the sauce and stir in gently. Carefully fold in the remaining egg whites with a metal spoon.

5 Pour into the dishes. Bake in the oven for 20–25 minutes, or until well risen and lightly set. Dust the tops with icing sugar before serving.

Black Cherry &
Chocolate Cake

Makes 10–12 slices

Butter, for greasing
Two 425g cans stoned black cherries,
   drained
125ml rum
6 eggs
200g caster sugar
150g self-raising flour
5 tablespoons cocoa powder
600ml double or whipping cream
3 tablespoons black cherry jam
115g plain chocolate, grated
8 dark red glacé cherries, to decorate

1 Preheat the oven to 200°C/400°F/Gas mark 6.
Grease and base-line two 23cm round sandwich
cake tins. Put the cherries in a large bowl and pour
over half of the rum. Set aside.

2 Put the eggs and sugar, less 3 tablespoons, in a
large heatproof bowl set over a saucepan of
simmering water. Using a hand-held electric mixer,
whisk for 15-20 minutes, or until the mixture is
pale, creamy and thick enough to leave a trail.

Remove from the heat. Sift the flour and cocoa
powder over the whisked egg mixture and fold in
gently but thoroughly.

3 Pour the mixture into the prepared tins,
dividing it evenly. Bake in the oven for
12-15 minutes, or until just firm to the touch.
Turn out on to a wire rack and leave to cool.

4 Whip the cream in a bowl until soft peaks
form. Whisk in the remaining rum and the
3 tablespoons of sugar. Brush each of the sponge
cakes with the rum that the cherries have been
soaking in, then spread the jam evenly over one of
the sponge cakes. Top this sponge cake with one-
third of the cream and the cherries. Place the other
sponge cake on top, then cover the top of the cake
with cream, reserving some for the decoration.

5 Sprinkle the top of the cake with the grated
chocolate, then pipe 8 rosettes of cream
around the top edge of the cake. Top with the
glacé cherries. Chill for 45 minutes before serving.

Cherry Cinnamon Cobbler

Serves 4–6

1kg stoned black cherries
  in heavy syrup
55g dried cherries
100g light brown sugar
2 tablespoons cornflour
2 tablespoons cold water

For the topping
200g plain flour
Pinch of salt
2 teaspoons baking powder
1 teaspoon ground cinnamon
100g brown sugar
85g butter, melted
120ml milk

1 Put a baking tray in the oven and preheat to 190°C/375°F/Gas mark 5. Drain the cherries, reserving the syrup. Put them with the dried cherries in a large pie dish. Pour 600ml of the syrup in a saucepan and add the brown sugar. Slowly bring to the boil, stirring continuously until the sugar has dissolved.

2 Mix the cornflour and cold water together in a small bowl and stir into the syrup. Cook for 1–2 minutes, or until the syrup thickens. Pour the syrup over the cherries.

3 For the topping, combine the flour, salt, baking powder, cinnamon and sugar in a bowl. Stir in the melted butter and milk and mix well. Spoon dollops of the mixture over the cherries.

4 Bake for 35–40 minutes, or until the topping is risen and golden.

Tip
A cobbler is fruit topped with a crust, which can be made from cookie dough, pie pastry, or biscuit topping, and baked.

Grape Pie

Serves 6

175g plain flour, plus extra for dusting
Pinch of salt
¼ teaspoon ground ginger
90g chilled butter, or half butter/half
  white vegetable fat
2 tablespoons cold water
1 tablespoon milk, for glazing
1 tablespoon demerara sugar, for
  sprinkling
Custard or cream, to serve

For the filling
675g white or red grapes, preferably
  seedless
50g demerara sugar, or to taste
2 tablespoons cornflour
3 tablespoons grape, apple or orange
  juice
1 tablespoon butter

1 Sift the flour, salt and ginger into a mixing bowl. Add the fat and rub it in until the mixture resembles fine breadcrumbs. Sprinkle over the water and mix to a firm dough. Knead briefly, then wrap in cling film and chill for 30 minutes. Meanwhile, preheat the oven to 200°C/400°F/ Gas mark 6.

2 For the filling, halve the grapes, if large, removing the pips if necessary, and put them in a bowl with the sugar. Blend the cornflour with the fruit juice and pour over the grapes, then toss the mixture gently with your hands to ensure all the fruit is coated.

3 Using an inverted 1 litre pie dish with a rim as a guide, roll out the pastry on a floured surface until it is 5cm larger all around than the dish. Cut off a 2.5cm strip from around the edge. Moisten the rim of the dish and position the strip on the rim. Brush with water.

4 Stir the grape mixture, and then tip into the pie dish, piling up the grapes in the centre so that the filling is slightly rounded. Dot the top of the fruit with butter. Place the pastry lid on top, pressing the edges together to seal. Trim off the excess pastry and snip a hole in the top of the pie to allow steam to escape.

5 Crimp the pastry edge. Brush with milk, then sprinkle with demerara sugar. Bake the pie for 15 minutes, then reduce the temperature to 180°C/350°F/Gas mark 4 and bake for a further 20–30 minutes, or until the pastry is golden brown. Serve hot or warm with custard or cream.

Deep-Dish Apple Pie à la Mode

Serves 4–6

215g plain flour, plus extra for dusting
½ teaspoon salt
115g butter
60ml ice water
Whisked egg white or cream, for glazing
Granulated sugar, or sprinkling
   (optional)
Ice cream, to serve

For the filling
675g peeled and cored tart apples,
   thinly sliced
1 tablespoon lemon juice
150g granulated sugar
50g brown sugar
2 tablespoons plain flour
⅛ teaspoon salt
¼ teaspoon freshly grated nutmeg
¼ teaspoon ground cinnamon
1 tablespoon butter

1 Preheat the oven to 230°C/450°F/Gas mark 8. For the pastry, sift the flour and salt into a mixing bowl. Add the butter and rub it in until the mixture resembles fine breadcrumbs. Slowly mix in the water with a fork until the dough forms a ball. Wrap in cling film and chill for 1 hour.

2 Divide the dough into 2 equal-sized balls. Dust the work surface and rolling pin lightly with flour. Flatten each ball of dough, sprinkle the surface with flour, roll from the centre into a round about 28cm in diameter. Place the first round in the base of a 25cm pie tin and gently press the dough into the sides of the tin.

3 Toss the apple slices in lemon juice to prevent them turning brown and arrange them closely together on top of the round of dough. Mix the two kinds of sugar, the flour, salt, nutmeg, cinnamon and butter in another bowl and sprinkle over the apples.

4 Lay the second round of dough loosely over the apples and fold the overhang under the edges of the dish to seal. Trim off the excess dough. Press firmly around the rim with the tines of a fork. Brush the surface with whisked egg white or cream. For a glistening, sugary top, sprinkle lightly with sugar.

5 Bake for 10 minutes on the lowest shelf in the oven, then reduce the temperature to 180°C/350°F/Gas mark 4 and bake for a further 30–45 minutes. The apples are done when juice bubbles from the steam vents and the fruit feels tender when skewered. Transfer the pie to a wire rack and leave to cool for 3 hours. Serve warm with ice cream.

Banoffee Pie

Serves 6–8

150g plain flour
115g chilled butter, finely diced
50g caster sugar

For the filling

115g butter
115g light brown sugar
2 tablespoons golden syrup
200g can sweetened
   condensed skimmed milk
2 medium bananas
1 tablespoon lemon juice
160ml double cream
55g plain chocolate,
   coarsely grated, to decorate

Tip

If you're not going
to eat the pie within the next
24 hours, place the bananas
before the toffee. This will stop
the banana going brown.
Cover with cream just
before serving.

1 Sift the flour into a bowl. Add the butter and rub it in until the mixture resembles coarse breadcrumbs. Stir in the sugar, then mix to a soft dough. Wrap in cling film and chill for 30 minutes.

2 Put a baking tray in the oven and preheat to 160°C/325°F/Gas mark 3. Press the pastry into a 20cm loose-bottomed tart tin. Prick the base with a fork, then chill for 10 minutes. Line the pastry case with greaseproof paper and fill with baking beans. Bake blind for 15 minutes. Remove the paper and beans and cook for 10 minutes until golden and crisp. Transfer to a wire rack to cool.

3 For the filling, put the butter in a saucepan over a low heat. When it starts to melt, add the sugar, golden syrup and condensed milk. Heat gently until the sugar has dissolved.

4 Bring to the boil then simmer for 8-10 minutes, stirring until it turns a light caramel colour. Cool for a few minutes, then pour into the pastry case and leave to cool completely.

5 Slice the bananas diagonally. Toss the slices in lemon juice, then arrange in concentric circles in the centre of the pie. Whip the cream until soft peaks form, then pipe swirls around the edge. Decorate with grated chocolate.

Two-Crust Prune Pie

Serves 6–8

225g plain flour, plus extra for dusting
Pinch of salt
½ teaspoon ground cinnamon
115g butter, or half butter/half white
   vegetable fat, diced
3–4 tablespoons cold water
1 tablespoon milk, for glazing
1 tablespoon caster sugar
Custard or cream, to serve

For the filling
450g dried prunes
1 tablespoon plain flour
50g caster sugar
2 teaspoons lemon juice
2 teaspoons butter

1 For the filling, put the prunes in a large bowl and pour over enough near-boiling water to just cover them. Leave to soak for 2 hours.

2 For the pastry, sift the flour, salt and cinnamon into a mixing bowl. Add the fat and rub it in until the mixture resembles fine breadcrumbs. Sprinkle 3 tablespoons water over the surface and mix to a firm dough. Knead briefly, then wrap in cling film and chill for 30 minutes.

3 Drain the prunes, reserving 240ml of the soaking liquid. Halve the prunes and remove the stones. Blend the flour, sugar, lemon juice and a little of the soaking liquid to a paste in a saucepan. Stir in the remaining soaking liquid, then add the prunes and butter. Bring to the boil and simmer for 1–2 minutes, or until thickened, stirring continuously. Remove from the heat and cool.

4 Put a baking tray in the oven and preheat to 190°C/375°F/Gas mark 5. Roll out two-thirds of the pastry on a lightly floured surface to a round about 4cm larger than a shallow 20–23cm pie dish. Ease the dough into the pie dish, leaving an overhang of pastry.

5 Spoon the prune mixture into the pastry case, then dampen the pastry edge with water. Roll out the remaining pastry to make a lid and use to cover the pie, pressing the edges together well to seal. Trim the excess pastry with a knife.

6 Crimp the edge of the pie, then decorate by cutting pastry leaves from the trimmings. Brush the pie with milk and sprinkle with sugar. Slash the top twice, or make small holes with a skewer to allow steam to escape. Bake for 35–40 minutes, or until the pastry is golden brown and crisp. Serve hot with custard or cream.

Peach Cobbler

Serves 4–6

1kg firm ripe peaches or nectarines
  (or canned equivalent)
3 teaspoons cornflour
115g caster sugar
¼ teaspoon ground cinnamon
Juice of 1 lemon
25g butter, diced
Custard or cream, to serve

For the topping
225g self-raising flour, plus extra
  for dusting
Pinch of salt
1 teaspoon baking powder
40g butter, diced
150ml milk
Beaten egg, for glazing
1 tablespoon icing sugar, for dusting

1 Preheat the oven to 160°C/325°F/Gas mark 3. For the filling, drop a few peaches at a time into a saucepan of boiling water, leave for 30–40 seconds, then transfer to a bowl of cold water. Peel and slice the fruit, removing the stones.

2 Put the fruit slices in a bowl. Blend the cornflour, sugar and cinnamon together, and sprinkle over. Gently toss together with the lemon juice, then transfer to a 23cm pie dish. Dot the top with butter. Cover with foil, then bake for 20 minutes.

3 For the pastry, sift the flour, salt and baking powder together into a mixing bowl. Add the butter and rub it in until the mixture resembles breadcrumbs. Stir in enough milk to give a fairly soft dough.

4 Remove the peaches from the oven and stir. Increase the temperature to 220°C/425°F/Gas mark 7. Roll out the dough on a lightly floured surface until slightly larger than the pie dish. Lightly brush the edges of the dish with water, then put the lid over the filling. Brush the top with beaten egg and make 2 small slits in the top. Bake for 12–15 minutes, or until the top is well risen and golden brown. Dust with icing sugar and serve hot with custard or cream.

Cranberry Pie

Serves 6

225g plain flour, plus extra for dusting
Pinch of salt
100g butter
2 tablespoons caster sugar, plus extra
   for topping
1 egg yolk
1–2 tablespoons milk
Whipped cream, to serve

For the filling
250g caster sugar
Finely grated zest and juice of
   1 orange
675g cranberries

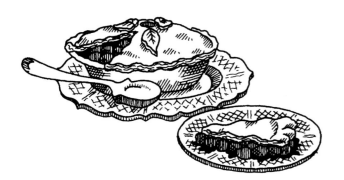

1 Preheat the oven to 200°C/400°F/Gas mark 6. Mix the flour and salt together in a bowl. Add the butter and rub it in until the mixture resembles breadcrumbs. Stir in the sugar, then add enough of the egg to make a dough. Wrap in cling film and leave to rest in a cool place for 30 minutes.

2 For the filling, mix the sugar, the grated orange zest and juice together in a bowl. Mix well, then stir in the cranberries. Spoon into a deep 1.5 litre pie dish.

3 Roll out the pastry on a lightly floured surface to fit the top of the dish, adding an extra 2.5cm all around. Cut off a 2.5cm strip from around the edge. Dampen the rim of the pie dish lightly with water and stick the pastry strip in place. Add the milk to any remaining egg yolk, and brush a little of this on to the pastry strip. Put the pastry lid on top, seal and crimp the edges.

4 Decorate the top of the pie with pastry shapes, if liked. Snip one or two holes in the top of the pie to allow the steam to escape, then brush the pastry with the remaining egg and milk mixture. Sprinkle with sugar. Bake the pie above the centre of the oven for 25-35 minutes, or until the pastry is golden and crisp. Sprinkle with more sugar and serve with whipped cream.

Key Lime Pie

Serves 6–8

75g butter, melted, plus extra for
  greasing
35 vanilla wafers or *langue de chat*
  biscuits
2–3 tablespoons caster sugar

For the filling
225g can sweetened condensed milk
125ml freshly squeezed limes
3 egg yolks

To decorate (optional)
240ml double cream, whipped
Zest of 1 lime

1 Lightly grease a 23cm pie dish. Put the wafers or biscuits in a strong plastic bag and crush with a rolling pin until very fine crumbs form. Alternatively, use a food processor. Put the crumbs into a large bowl, add the sugar and butter and mix well.

2 Pour the crumbs into the prepared pie dish and, using the back of the spoon, press the crumbs evenly onto the base and side of the plate. Leave to chill.

3 For the filling, whisk the condensed milk, lime juice and egg yolks together in a bowl until well blended and thickened. Pour into the pie case and leave to chill until set. Decorate with a little whipped cream and lime zest, if liked. Serve with additional whipped cream.

Tip
This is best served very cold, so place it in the freezer for 15–20 minutes before serving.

Blackberry & Apple Pie

Serves 6–8

375g plain flour, plus extra for dusting
55g icing sugar
125g butter
1 egg, plus 1 egg yolk
Milk, for glazing
Caster sugar, for sprinkling

For the filling
3 small tart apples, peeled, cored
   and thinly sliced
700g blackberries
200g granulated sugar
1 tablespoon cornflour
½ teaspoon ground allspice
½ teaspoon freshly grated nutmeg

1 Sift the flour and icing sugar into a mixing bowl. Add the butter and rub it in until the mixture resembles breadcrumbs. Add the egg and egg yolk, and mix quickly to a rough dough. Wrap in cling film and leave to rest in a cool place, not the refrigerator, for 20 minutes.

2 Put a baking tray in the oven and preheat to 200°C/400°F/Gas mark 6. Put the apple slices in a bowl, add the blackberries, sugar, cornflour, allspice and nutmeg and toss gently to mix.

3 Roll out just less than half the pastry on a lightly floured surface and use to line a 25cm pie dish. Spoon the filling on top.

4 Roll out the remaining dough to a round 2.5cm wider than the rim of the dish. Moisten the rim of the pastry case with water, then place the pastry on top. Seal and trim off the excess pastry. Crimp the edges and snip a hole in the top to allow steam to escape. Brush the pie with milk and sprinkle with sugar.

5 Bake for 15 minutes, then reduce the oven temperature to 180°C/350°F/Gas mark 4 and bake for a further 20–25 minutes. Serve warm.

Cherry Strudel

Serves 8

4 large sheets filo pastry, thawed if
  frozen
50g unsalted butter, melted
Icing sugar, for dusting

For the filling
550g fresh black cherries,
  stoned and halved
40g ground almonds
90g granulated sugar
55g fresh cake crumbs

1 Preheat the oven to 190°C/375°F/Gas mark 5. For the filling, put the cherries, ground almonds, granulated sugar and cake crumbs in a bowl and stir to combine.

2 Cover the filo pastry with a damp tea towel to prevent it drying out. Lay a sheet of the pastry on a large, flat baking tray and brush with a little melted butter. Lay a second sheet over the top and brush with butter. Repeat this twice more so that you have a rectangle of 4 sheets of pastry.

3 Spoon the cherry mixture over the top, leaving a gap of 5cm around the edge. Roll up the longest side – like you would a Swiss roll. Tuck in the ends and form into a horseshoe shape.

4 Brush the surface of the pastry with more butter and bake for 25 minutes. Dust with icing sugar and serve warm or at room temperature.

Linzertorte with a Lattice Top

Serves 8

225g plain flour, plus extra for dusting
Pinch of salt
50g ground almonds
150g unsalted butter, diced
4 tablespoons golden brown sugar
2 eggs, separated
3–4 teaspoons cold water
Icing sugar, for dusting
Double cream, to serve

For the filling
450g fresh raspberries
100g caster sugar
2 teaspoons cornflour mixed
  with 2 teaspoons cold water
1 tablespoon fresh lemon juice

1 Mix the flour, salt and ground almonds in a mixing bowl. Add the butter and rub it in until the mixture resembles fine breadcrumbs. Stir in the golden brown sugar. Mix the egg yolks with the cold water. Add to the pastry and bring the dough together. Knead briefly until smooth. Wrap in cling film and chill for 30 minutes.

2 Put the raspberries and sugar into a saucepan over a low heat. Bring to the boil, stir in the cornflour mixture and cook for 2 minutes. Remove from the heat, stir in the lemon juice and leave until cold.

3 Put a baking tray in the oven and preheat to 200°C/400°F/Gas mark 6. Roll out two-thirds of the pastry on a lightly floured surface. Roll the pastry into a round at least 5cm larger than a deep, loose-bottomed 20cm fluted tart tin. Gently roll the pastry onto the rolling pin, then unroll it over the tin to cover. Carefully press the pastry into the edge of the tin, removing any overhanging pastry. Prick the base all over with a fork. Chill for 20 minutes.

4 Roll the pastry trimmings with the remaining pastry. Cut into 10 long strips, each 2cm wide using a zigzag cutter. Spoon the raspberry mixture into the pastry case. Dampen the edges of the pastry using the egg white, then lay the strips over the top of the filling to make a lattice pattern. Gently press the edges of the pastry together, and trim off the excess.

5 Bake for 35–40 minutes until the pastry is golden. Leave to cool for 5 minutes. Remove from the tin and leave to stand for 10–15 minutes. Dust with icing sugar and serve warm with cream.

Hot Waffles & Banana
with Toffee Brandy Sauce

Serves 2

2 waffles
2 scoops vanilla ice cream
2 bananas, sliced

For the sauce
60ml double cream
25g molasses sugar
45g butter
2 tablespoons brandy

1 For the sauce, put the cream, sugar, butter and brandy in a small saucepan and heat gently until the sugar has dissolved. Increase the heat and simmer for 3 minutes, or until thickened.

2 Warm the waffles in the microwave, or heat in the oven or toaster according to the instructions on the packet. Put a generous scoop of ice cream and half the sliced bananas on each one. Drizzle over the sauce and serve.

Swiss Roll
with Lemon Cream

Serves 6

4 large eggs
100g caster sugar, plus extra
    for dusting
100g plain flour
Sifted icing sugar and finely grated
    lemon zest, to decorate

For the filling
250g mascarpone cheese
Finely grated zest and juice of ½ lemon
2 tablespoons freshly squeezed
    orange juice
4 tablespoons icing sugar

1 Preheat the oven to 220°C/425°F/Gas mark 7. Grease and line a 23 x 33cm Swiss roll tin.

2 For the sponge, using a hand-held electric mixer, whisk the eggs and sugar together in a large bowl until the mixture is pale, creamy and thick enough to leave a trail on the surface when the whisk is lifted.

3 Sift and fold in the flour in three batches. Pour the mixture into the prepared tin, tilting the tin backwards and forwards to spread evenly. Bake in the oven for about 10 minutes, or until risen and golden and the cake springs back when lightly pressed.

4 While the cake is cooking, lay a sheet of greaseproof paper on a work surface and sprinkle liberally with caster sugar.

5 Quickly turn the hot cake out onto the sugar-dusted paper and remove the lining paper. Trim off the crusty edges, score a cut 1cm in from one of the shorter ends, then roll up the cake from the scored short end with the paper inside. Place on a wire rack and leave to cool.

6 For the filling, put all the filling ingredients in a bowl and beat together until smooth and well mixed. Carefully unroll the cake, remove the paper and spread the filling mixture evenly over the cake. Re-roll the cake. To decorate, sprinkle the cake with sifted icing sugar and lemon zest. Serve in slices.

Crumb Pie

Serves 6

115g plain flour, plus extra for dusting
Pinch of salt
50g butter, diced
1 egg yolk
1½ tablespoons cold water

For the topping
40g plain flour
75g cake crumbs
1 teaspoon ground cinnamon
Pinch of freshly grated nutmeg
Pinch of ground ginger
75g butter

For the filling
150g light brown sugar
75ml hot water
2 eggs, lightly beaten
75g raisins

1 Sift the flour and salt into a mixing bowl. Add the butter and rub it in until the mixture resembles breadcrumbs. Mix the egg yolk and water together in another bowl. Add all but 2 teaspoons of the egg mixture and mix to a firm dough. Knead until smooth, wrap in cling film and chill for 30 minutes.

2 Preheat the oven to 200°C/400°F/Gas mark 6. Roll out the pastry on a lightly floured surface and use to line a 20cm tart tin. Prick the base all over, then chill for 15 minutes. Line the pastry case with greaseproof paper and fill with baking beans. Bake for 15 minutes. Remove the paper and beans, brush the base with the reserved egg and bake for a further 5 minutes. Reduce the oven temperature to 160°C/325°F/Gas mark 3.

3 For the topping, sift the flour into a bowl and stir in the cake crumbs and spices. Add the butter and rub it in until the mixture resembles coarse breadcrumbs. Set aside.

4 For the filling, put the sugar, hot water and eggs into a bowl set over a saucepan of simmering water, stirring for 7-8 minutes until the mixture thickens. Sprinkle the raisins over the base of the pastry case, then pour in the filling. Sprinkle over the crumb mixture and bake for 20-25 minutes, or until lightly set.

Baked Apples with Walnut Jackets

Makes 14

120g walnuts
4 gingersnaps, broken
180g soft light brown sugar
1 teaspoon ground cinnamon
½ teaspoon Chinese five spice powder
4 large cooking apples
3 tablespoons butter, melted
Natural yoghurt, to serve

1 Preheat the oven to 180°C/350°F/Gas mark 4. Blend the walnuts, gingersnaps, brown sugar, cinnamon and five spice powder in a food processor or blender until the mixture forms fine crumbs.

2 Core the apples, then score the skin on each one around the circumference, two-thirds of the way down the fruit. Peel off all the skin above the mark. Take a thin slice off the bottom of each apple, if necessary, so that they stand straight.

3 Put the apples in a baking dish and fill each one with the walnut mixture, packing it down firmly. Brush the exposed flesh on the top of each apple with the butter and press the remaining walnut mixture onto it so that each apple is topped with a walnut jacket. Drizzle any remaining butter over, being careful not to dislodge the crust.

4 Bake the apples for 45 minutes or until tender. Serve hot or cold with natural yoghurt.

Banana & Toffee

Cheesecake

Serves 10–12

225g plain flour, plus extra for dusting
Pinch of salt
115g butter, diced
50g caster sugar
3–4 tablespoons cold water

For the filling
115g plain chocolate, melted,
    plus extra to decorate
3 large ripe but firm bananas,
    thickly sliced
Juice of ½ lemon
250g mascarpone cheese
150ml double cream, lightly whipped
450g jar thick toffee or caramel
    sauce/spread

1 Sift the flour and salt into a mixing bowl. Add the butter and rub it in until the mixture resembles coarse breadcrumbs. Stir in the sugar. Add 3 tablespoons cold water and mix to a dough. Knead briefly until the dough is smooth. Shape into a ball, wrap in cling film and chill for 20 minutes.

2 Roll out the pastry on a lightly floured surface to form a round at least 5cm larger than a 23cm plain pastry ring set on a baking tray. Use the pastry round to line the ring, pressing the edges and trimming the overhanging pastry. Prick the base with a fork. Chill for 20 minutes.

3 Preheat the oven to 200°C/400°F/Gas mark 6. Line the pastry case with greaseproof paper and fill with baking beans and bake in the oven for 12 minutes. Remove the paper and beans and bake for a further 10-12 minutes, or until golden. Remove from the oven and leave to cool. Using a pastry brush, paint the inside of the pastry case with melted chocolate. Chill until set.

4 For the cheesecake, toss the bananas in the lemon juice and set aside. Beat the mascarpone cheese in a bowl until softened, then stir in the whipped cream. Carefully fold the cream mixture and most of the caramel sauce together (reserving a little sauce for decoration), leaving them marbled. Spoon the mixture into the pastry case, then scatter the banana over the top. Drizzle the remaining caramel over the bananas. Chill before serving.

CHOCOLATE HEAVEN

- Mississippi Mud Pie
- Chocolate Cream Pie
- Chocolate Espresso Pots
- Chocolate Brioche Pudding
- Chocolate Raspberry Torte
- Chocolate & Orange Mousse
- White & Dark Chocolate Cheesecake with Raspberries
- Chocolate & Chestnut Vacherin
- Marshmallow & Chocolate Ice Cream
- Rich Mocha Pots
- Bitter Chocolate Sorbet
- Rich Chocolate Tartlets
- Chocolate Marquise with Vanilla Crème Anglaise
- Chocolate Fudge Cake
- Marshmallow & Chocolate Pie
- Chocolate Doughnuts
- White Chocolate Parfait
- Kahlua & Chocolate Trifle
- Chocolate Crêpes with Caramelized Bananas & Cream
- Chocolate & Toffee Tart
- Chocolate Tiramisù
- Cappuccino Truffle Cake
- Chocolate Amaretto Cheesecake
- Chocolate Pudding
- Peppermint Chocolate Layer Cake
- Double Chocolate Chunky Brownies
- Super-quick Bailey's Chocolate Mousse
- Chocolate & Brandy Truffles
- Chocolate Layer Cake

CHAPTER TWO

CHOCOLATE
HEAVEN

Mississippi Mud Pie

Serves 6–8

75g butter, softened
140g plain flour
2 tablespoons iced water
75g chopped walnuts
115g icing sugar
225g tub cream cheese, softened
500ml double cream, whipped
175g packet instant chocolate
    pudding mix
1 litre milk
1 heaped teaspoon cocoa powder

To decorate
Sifted cocoa powder
Chopped nuts

1 Preheat the oven to 180°C/350°F/Gas mark 4. Put the butter and flour in a mixing bowl and rub together lightly until the mixture resembles fine breadcrumbs. Stir in the water. Distribute the walnuts through the mixture, then press the mixture into a 23cm pie dish. Bake for 12-15 minutes. Remove from the oven and leave to cool.

2 Combine the icing sugar, cream cheese and 225g of the whipped cream, reserving the rest for the topping in another bowl. Gently spread the mixture over the first cooked layer. Chill while you prepare the pudding mix with the milk, according to the instructions on the packet, in a separate bowl. Mix in the cocoa powder. Remove the chilled pie from the refrigerator and spread the chocolate pudding mix over the second layer. Top with the reserved whipped cream, dust with a fine layer of cocoa powder and sprinkle with chopped nuts. Chill for a further 4 hours before serving.

Chocolate Cream Pie

Serves 6–8

175g plain flour, plus extra for dusting
2 tablespoons caster sugar
115g butter, diced
1 egg yolk
2–3 teaspoons cold water
Chocolate curls, to decorate

For the filling
50g cornflour
90g caster sugar
160ml single cream
275ml milk
90g plain chocolate, broken into pieces
2 egg yolks
2 tablespoons butter

For the topping
240ml double cream
½ teaspoon vanilla extract
2 teaspoons icing sugar, sifted

1 Sift the flour and sugar into a mixing bowl. Add the butter and rub it in until the mixture resembles fine breadcrumbs. Mix the egg yolk and 2 teaspoons water together and sprinkle over the dry ingredients. Mix to a dough, adding extra water if needed. Knead, cover and chill for 30 minutes.

2 Put a baking sheet in the oven and preheat to 200°C/400°F/Gas mark 6. Roll out the pastry on a lightly floured surface and use to line a shallow 20–23cm pie dish. Chill for 10 minutes. Line the pastry case with greaseproof paper and fill with baking beans. Bake blind for 15 minutes. Remove the paper and beans and cook for 8–10 minutes until golden and crisp. Cool on a wire rack.

3 Mix the cornflour and sugar together in a non-stick saucepan. Gradually blend in the cream, then stir in the milk and chocolate. Gently heat, stirring, until the chocolate melts and the mixture thickens and boils. Remove from the heat.

4 Beat the egg yolks. Stir in a few spoonfuls of the chocolate mixture, then pour and stir the egg mixture back into the chocolate mixture in the pan. Continue to stir for 1 minute, but do not boil. Remove from the heat and stir in the butter. Cool slightly, then pour into the pastry case. Press a circle of dampened baking paper on top. Cool, then chill for 2 hours. Remove the paper.

5 For the topping, pour the cream into a chilled bowl. Stir in the vanilla and sugar. Whip until soft peaks form, then spoon into a piping bag with a large star nozzle and pipe a lattice pattern on top. Scatter with chocolate curls and serve.

Chocolate Espresso Pots

Serves 8

175g plain chocolate, 70 per cent cocoa
   solids, broken into pieces, plus a
   little extra to decorate
300ml strong, fresh espresso coffee
2 tablespoons coffee liqueur or whisky
50g caster sugar
6 egg yolks
50ml double cream, to serve

1 Put the chocolate into a heatproof bowl along
with the coffee and coffee liqueur or whisky.
Set the bowl over a saucepan of simmering water.
The bowl should not touch the water. Leave,
without stirring, until the chocolate has melted,
then stir until smooth. Remove from the heat
and stir in the sugar. Leave to cool for about
5 minutes.

2 Beat in the egg yolks, then pour the mixture
through a sieve into 8 small espresso cups
or ramekins. Leave to cool, then chill for at least
4 hours, or overnight.

3 When ready to serve, lightly whip the cream
and put a spoonful on top of each chocolate
cup. Sprinkle over a little extra grated chocolate
and serve.

Tip

Chocolate should always be
heated in a heatproof bowl set over a
saucepan of simmering water so that the
heat doesn't burn the chocolate. Put half of
the chocolate in a heatproof bowl, and stir
with a spatula when the outside edges of the
chocolate begin to melt. Gradually add the
rest of the chocolate. When it has almost
melted remove the bowl from the heat,
and continue stirring until the
chocolate is smooth
and shiny.

Chocolate Brioche Pudding

Serves 8

400g brioche loaf
75g unsalted butter, softened
200g plain chocolate
300ml whipping cream
450ml ready-made custard
225ml milk

1 Using a serrated bread knife, cut the crusts off the brioche loaf, then cut into 1cm slices. Grease a 23cm square gratin dish with a little of the butter then sparingly spread the remaining butter over the brioche. Lay half the slices over the base of the dish.

2 Put half the chocolate on a board and roughly chop with a large sharp knife. Sprinkle evenly over the brioche, then top with the remaining buttered slices. Finely chop the remaining chocolate. Bring the cream to the boil in a small saucepan, add the chocolate and stir until melted.

3 Whisk the custard and milk together and stir in the chocolate cream. Pour over the brioche and leave to soak for 30 minutes. Preheat the oven to 150°C/300°F/Gas mark 2. Put the dish in a roasting tin and pour enough hot water to come halfway up the side of the dish. Cook in the oven for about 55 minutes. It should be firm with a little wobble. Leave the pudding to stand for 5 minutes before serving.

Chocolate Raspberry Torte

Serves 6–8

40g unsalted butter, plus extra for
   greasing
50g plain flour
4 tablespoons cocoa powder, plus extra
   for dusting
3 large eggs
75g caster sugar
425ml double cream
4 tablespoons orange liqueur
175g fresh or frozen raspberries
1 tablespoon icing sugar
50g plain chocolate, grated

1 Grease and line a 23cm round cake tin. Preheat the oven to 180°C/350°F/Gas mark 4. Sift the flour and cocoa together and melt the butter. Break the eggs into a bowl and add the caster sugar. Put the bowl over a saucepan of hot water and whisk with an electric hand-held whisk until pale and the yolk falls from the whisk in a thick 'ribbon'.

2 Sift the flour and cocoa in 3 batches over the eggs and gently fold in, drizzling a little butter around the bowl in between each batch. Discard any white sediment at the base of the pan.

3 Pour into the prepared tin and bake for 20 minutes until brown and the top springs back when pressed lightly. Leave to cool in the tin for 2–3 minutes, then turn out on to a wire rack to cool completely.

4 For the filling, whip the cream and liqueur until the mixture forms soft peaks. Fold in the raspberries, sugar and chocolate.

5 Cut the cake through horizontally to make two layers. Line a 20cm springform tin with baking paper and trim the cake to fit the base of the tin. Put one of the cake halves at the bottom. Pile in the raspberry cream and top with the remaining cake. Press down evenly and freeze for 4 hours until the filling is firm. Dust the top with cocoa then remove from the tin and serve in slices.

Tip
To cut the torte into clean wedges, wipe the knife between slices.

Chocolate & Orange Mousse

Serves 4

225g good-quality plain chocolate,
   broken into pieces
Grated zest and juice of 1 large orange
1 tablespoon Grand Marnier
4 eggs, separated
55g icing sugar
150ml double cream
Pared strips of orange zest, to decorate
   (optional)

1 Put the chocolate in a heatproof bowl. Add the orange zest and juice and the Grand Marnier and set over a saucepan of simmering water. Heat until the chocolate has melted, then stir until smooth. Leave to cool.

2 Whisk the egg yolks and icing sugar together until the mixture becomes pale and frothy. Stir into the cooled chocolate mixture.

3 Lightly whip the cream and fold into the mousse mixture. Whisk the egg whites in a clean, grease-free bowl until soft peaks form and carefully fold into the mixture. Pour into 4 custard cups, individual ramekins, a soufflé dish or a glass bowl and leave to chill for 3–4 hours until set. Decorate with orange zest, if liked.

White & Dark Chocolate

Cheesecake with Raspberries

Serves 2

75g digestive biscuits, crushed
45g unsalted butter, melted
1 tablespoon cocoa powder

For the filling
75g white chocolate
75g full-fat cream cheese
6 tablespoons crème fraîche or soured
  cream
2 tablespoons icing sugar

To decorate
75g raspberries
25g plain chocolate curls or grated
  plain chocolate
1 tablespoon cocoa powder, for dusting

1 Mix the digestive biscuits, butter and cocoa together in a bowl. Use two 8cm round biscuit cutters to shape the base. Place the cutters on a flat plate and divide the biscuits between each of them. Press down on the biscuits until firmly packed. Alternatively, you can line the base of two large ramekins with the biscuit base. Put in the refrigerator to chill while you make the filling.

2 Melt the chocolate in a bowl set over a saucepan of simmering water. Beat all the ingredients together for the filling and pour on top of the bases. Chill for 2 hours, or until firm. Lift off the biscuit cutters, top with raspberries, chocolate curls or grated chocolate and dust with cocoa.

Chocolate & Chestnut

Vacherin

Serves 8–10

5 egg whites
275g caster sugar
2 teaspoons vanilla extract
400ml double cream
300g plain chocolate, broken
   into pieces
225g unsweetened chestnut purée
3 tablespoons brandy
120g icing sugar, sifted
1 tablespoon cocoa powder, sifted,
   to decorate

1 Preheat the oven to 120°C/250°F/Gas mark ½. Line 3 baking trays with greaseproof paper. Draw a circle around the base of a 20cm cake tin on each piece of paper.

2 Whisk the egg whites in a clean, grease-free bowl until stiff peaks form. Beat in the sugar a tablespoon at a time – the mixture should be stiff and glossy. Fold in the vanilla extract.

3 Spoon equal quantities of meringue mixture into the middle of each circle and spread out evenly to the edges. Bake for 2 hours, then peel off the paper and leave to cool on wire racks.

4 Heat the cream in a saucepan until almost boiling. Remove from the heat and add the chocolate, stirring, until it has melted. Leave to cool, then chill for about 45 minutes, or until the mixture starts to thicken. Using an electric whisk, beat the chocolate mixture for 2-3 minutes until light and airy.

5 Mix the chestnut purée with the brandy and icing sugar. Spread half of the chocolate cream over the base of one meringue disc, then spread half of the chestnut mixture over the chocolate. Put a second meringue disc on top and repeat with the remaining chocolate and chestnut mixture. Top with the remaining meringue and dust with cocoa.

Marshmallow & Chocolate

Ice Cream

Serves 8

250g milk chocolate, broken into
  pieces
200g marshmallows
3 tablespoons water
400g carton fresh custard
300ml double cream

1 Put the chocolate in a heatproof bowl with three-quarters of the marshmallows. Add the water and set the bowl over a saucepan of gently simmering water. Melt the chocolate and stir until smooth, then leave to cool a little.

2 Stir the cooled chocolate mixture into the fresh custard. Chop the remaining marshmallows and fold into the mixture. Lightly whip the cream and fold in. Pour the mixture into a 1.2 litre terrine or loaf tin and freeze until hard. You may want to line the base of the terrine or tin with non-stick baking paper to make it easier to unmould.

3 To serve, dip the base of the terrine or tin in hot water and invert on to a serving plate. Cut the ice cream into thick slices.

Rich Mocha Pots

Makes 6–8 pots

175g plain chocolate, broken into
    pieces
3 tablespoons strong black coffee
15g butter
4 eggs, separated
2 tablespoons brandy
4 tablespoons icing sugar
Whipped cream
Grated chocolate or curls,
    to decorate

Tip
To make the chocolate
curls, run a vegetable
peeler along the edge of
a bar of chocolate.

1 Melt the chocolate in a bowl set over a saucepan of hot water. Stir in the coffee and butter until smooth. Remove from the heat and whisk in the egg yolks one by one until the mixture is smooth and glossy. Whisk in the brandy, then set aside to cool and thicken slightly while you are whisking the egg whites.

2 Whisk the egg whites in a clean, grease-free bowl until stiff. Gradually add the sugar and continue whisking until glossy and thick. Fold into the cooled chocolate mixture.

3 Pour into 6 or 8 small teacups or ramekins and chill for 3-4 hours until firm. Top with whipped cream and decorate with grated chocolate or chocolate curls.

Bitter Chocolate Sorbet

Serves 4

225g plain chocolate
225g granulated sugar
25g cocoa powder
500ml water

Tip

For a smooth product, process the sorbet mixture once during freezing and refreeze. This technique breaks up ice crystals. Sorbet melts quickly at room temperature, so serve quickly.

1 Put the chocolate in a food processor or blender and process until finely chopped. Put the sugar, cocoa and water in a saucepan and slowly bring to the boil, stirring, to dissolve the sugar. Bring to the boil, then simmer for 5 minutes.

2 Pour the chocolate syrup into the food processor and process until the mixture is completely smooth and the chocolate has melted. Pour into a shallow container and leave to cool. Once cool, put in the freezer to harden for 2-3 hours. Process until smooth in the food processor. Return to the container and freeze until hard.

Rich Chocolate Tartlets

Makes 6

350g ready-made sweet shortcrust
   pastry
Plain flour, for dusting
100g plain chocolate
2 eggs
20g caster sugar
150ml double cream

Tip
The pastry always needs to rest before baking to help prevent shrinkage during cooking.

1 Preheat the oven to 200°C/400°F/Gas mark 6. Divide the pastry into six pieces. Roll out each piece thinly on a lightly floured surface and use to line six individual tartlet tins. Chill for 20 minutes. Prick the bases and line with greaseproof paper and baking beans. Bake blind for 15 minutes.

2 Remove the paper and beans and bake for a further 5 minutes. Remove from the oven and set aside. Reduce the oven temperature to 190°C/375°F/Gas mark 5.

3 Melt the chocolate in a bowl set over a saucepan of simmering water. Stir, then leave to cool slightly. Whisk the eggs and sugar in another bowl until pale. Whisk in the cream, then the melted chocolate. Pour the chocolate mixture into the tartlet cases and bake for 15 minutes until set.

Chocolate Marquise with
Vanilla Crème Anglaise

Serves 6–8

300g bitter plain chocolate, broken
  into pieces
60ml very strong coffee
120g butter
120g caster sugar
4 egg yolks
400ml double cream

For the vanilla crème anglaise
300ml milk
1 vanilla pod, split
4 egg yolks
120g caster sugar

1 Line a 22 x 12 x 6cm loaf tin or terrine dish with cling film. Put the chocolate and coffee in a heatproof bowl set over a saucepan of simmering water and heat until the chocolate has melted. Stir, then leave to cool.

2 Beat the butter with 75g of the sugar until pale and fluffy. Whisk the egg yolks with the remaining sugar in another bowl until thickened and pale. Lightly whip the cream in a separate bowl until it just begins to hold its shape.

3 Beat the melted chocolate into the butter and fold in the egg yolk mixture, followed by the cream. Pour into the loaf tin and chill for 5-6 hours.

4 For the crème anglaise, bring the milk to the boil with the vanilla pod. Beat the egg yolks and sugar together. Add the hot milk, then return the mixture to the pan and stir over a low heat until it starts to thicken. Cool, then scrape out the seeds from the vanilla pod and stir into the cold custard. Chill until ready to serve.

5 To serve, turn the mousse out onto a serving plate and serve with the vanilla crème anglaise.

Chocolate Fudge Cake

Serves 8

175g unsalted butter, plus extra
  for greasing
250g plain chocolate,
  broken into pieces
4 tablespoons water
175g soft brown sugar
4 eggs, beaten
125g self-raising flour
75g ground almonds

For the filling
75g cocoa powder
175g soft brown sugar
50g icing sugar
175g unsalted butter, melted
4 tablespoons boiling water

For the icing
125g plain chocolate
50g unsalted butter
25g milk chocolate, melted (optional)

1 Preheat the oven to 180°C/350°F/Gas mark 4. Grease and base-line two 18cm cake tins. Melt the chocolate with the water in a bowl set over a saucepan of simmering water. Leave to cool slightly.

2 Cream the butter and sugar together until light and fluffy. Gradually add the beaten eggs. Stir in the melted chocolate, then fold in the flour and ground almonds. Pour into the prepared cake tins.

3 Bake for 25 minutes. Leave to cool a little, then turn out both cake halves on to a wire rack. With a long sharp knife, slice them through the middle horizontally so you have four layers.

4 For the filling, mix the cocoa powder, brown sugar and icing sugar together. Beat in the melted butter and stir in the water to make a smooth paste. Leave to harden in the refrigerator for about 20 minutes, then spread evenly over three layers of the cake and sandwich together. Put the final cake layer on top.

5 For the icing, melt the plain chocolate and butter together in a bowl set over a saucepan of simmering water. Beat until glossy then leave to cool until you have a spreading consistency. Smooth evenly over the top of the cake. Drizzle melted milk chocolate over in zigzag patterns, if liked.

Marshmallow
& Chocolate Pie

Serves 8–10

175g digestive biscuits, crushed to
   fine crumbs
85g unsalted butter, melted

For the filling
580g cream cheese
120g caster sugar
1 teaspoon vanilla extract
3 eggs, beaten
2 egg yolks
115g mini marshmallows

For the topping
300ml double cream
150g plain chocolate, broken into
   small pieces

1 Mix the digestive biscuits and melted butter together in a bowl, then press into the base of a 23cm springform cake tin. Chill for 30 minutes, or until firm. Wrap the outside of the tin in foil. Meanwhile, put a baking tray in the oven and preheat to 180°C/350°F/Gas mark 4.

2 To make the filling, mix the cream cheese, sugar and vanilla extract together in a bowl. Beat in the eggs and egg yolks, then fold in the marshmallows. Spoon the mixture into the cake tin and level the top.

3 Put the pie in a roasting tin half-full of boiling water and bake for 50 minutes. Leave to cool, then chill for 2–3 hours, or until firm.

4 For the topping, put the cream in a saucepan and bring to boiling point. Remove from the heat and stir in the chocolate until smooth. Cool for 10 minutes, then pour the sauce over the pie. Chill until the chocolate has set.

Chocolate Doughnuts

Makes 8

225g plain flour, plus extra for dusting
7g fast-action dried yeast
Pinch of salt
4 tablespoons caster sugar
25g butter, plus extra for greasing
150ml milk
2 egg yolks
Vegetable oil, for deep-frying
50g milk chocolate, broken into pieces

1 Mix the flour, yeast and salt together in a mixing bowl. Add the sugar, then add the butter and rub it in until the mixture resembles fine breadcrumbs.

2 Heat the milk in a saucepan until it is warm, then whisk in the egg yolks. Add the liquid to the flour mixture and mix to a soft dough. Cover with cling film and leave in a warm place to prove for about 1 hour, or until the dough has doubled in size.

3 Grease a large baking tray. Knock back the dough and knead on a well-floured surface for 5-10 minutes. Roll out the dough until 1cm thick, and stamp out rounds with a plain pastry cutter. Make a hole in the middle of each round with your finger. Put the doughnuts on the baking sheet and leave for 40 minutes–1 hour until doubled in size.

4 Heat the oil in a large, deep saucepan to 190°C/375°F and deep-fry the doughnuts one at a time for about 5 minutes, or until golden brown. Drain on kitchen paper and leave to cool.

5 Put the milk chocolate in a heatproof bowl set over a saucepan of simmering water. Heat until melted, then remove from the heat. Stir, then leave to cool lightly. Dip the rounded tops of the doughnuts in the melted chocolate and leave to set.

White Chocolate Parfait

Serves 4

175g white chocolate, broken
into pieces
2 tablespoons milk
1 vanilla pod
4 egg yolks
75g icing sugar
300ml whipping cream

To serve
Rich chocolate sauce
Fresh fruit

Tip
Always cover ice cream
when storing in the
freezer so it does not
absorb flavours from
other foods.

1 Melt the chocolate with the milk in a bowl set over a saucepan of gently simmering water. Stir until smooth, then leave to cool.

2 Split the vanilla pod lengthways and scrape out the seeds. Mix the seeds with the egg yolks and icing sugar, then beat with an electric whisk until light and fluffy. Stir in the melted chocolate.

3 Lightly whip the cream and fold into the mixture. Divide the mousse among four ramekins or dariole moulds and freeze for at least 4 hours until hard.

4 To serve, briefly dip the base of the moulds into warm water and turn out on to serving plates. Serve with rich chocolate sauce and fresh fruit.

Kahlua Chocolate Trifle

Serves 4–6

Butter, for greasing
150ml strong fresh coffee
4 tablespoons Kahlua or other coffee
   liqueur
175g shop-bought sponge fingers
500g mascarpone cheese
75g caster sugar
2 teaspoons vanilla extract
300ml double cream
100g plain chocolate, grated
Cocoa powder, for dusting

1 Grease and line a 900g loaf tin with cling film. Mix the coffee and liqueur together in a bowl. Dip the sponge fingers into the mixture and use some to line the base of the tin.

2 Put the mascarpone into a large bowl, then whisk in the sugar and vanilla extract. Add the cream a little at a time, whisking on a slow speed until smooth.

3 Spoon half of the mixture on top of the sponge fingers in the tin and spread over evenly. Add half the grated chocolate, then repeat a layer of the dipped sponge fingers, the remaining creamed mixture, grated chocolate and a final layer of dipped sponge fingers. Drizzle any remaining coffee mixture over the top.

4 Cover with a layer of cling film, then chill for 2-3 hours. Remove from the tin and peel off the cling film. Dust with a generous amount of cocoa powder, slice and serve.

Chocolate Crêpes with
Caramelized Bananas & Cream

Makes 10 crêpes

150g plain flour
2 tablespoons cocoa powder
2 tablespoons caster sugar
2 eggs, beaten
200ml milk
100ml water
1 tablespoon sunflower oil, plus extra
   for frying
4 bananas, sliced
50g icing sugar
300ml double cream, whipped

1 Mix the flour, cocoa powder and caster sugar together in a large bowl. Add the beaten eggs and slowly pour in the milk and water, beating until you have a smooth batter. Stir in the oil, then leave to rest for 30 minutes.

2 Brush a large crêpe pan with a little oil and put over a medium heat. Pour in a ladleful of batter and fry until set. Flip the crêpe over and quickly fry the other side. Set aside and keep warm. Repeat with the remaining batter.

3 For the filling, preheat the grill. Put the sliced bananas on to a non-stick baking tray. Sprinkle with the icing sugar and cook under the grill for 3–4 minutes until golden. Fill each crêpe with a few banana slices, and top with a spoonful of whipped cream. Fold the crêpes in half or quarters and serve immediately.

Tip
Pancakes are ready to flip when their surface is covered with bubbles, their edges look dry and a peek at their undersides reveals a golden brown colour. Turn them gently, barely lifting them off the pan.

Chocolate & Toffee Tart

Serves 6–8

275g plain flour, plus extra for dusting
Pinch of salt
25g icing sugar
175g unsalted butter, diced
2 egg yolks
4 tablespoons cold water
Cocoa powder, for dusting

For the filling
125ml water
350g caster sugar
125g golden syrup
240g unsalted butter
250ml double cream
1 teaspoon vanilla extract
115g plain chocolate, at least 50 per
 cent cocoa, grated

1 Sift the flour, salt and icing sugar into a mixing bowl. Add the butter and rub it in until the mixture resembles breadcrumbs. Whisk the egg yolks with the cold water. Make a well in the centre of the flour and pour in the egg mixture and mix together to form a dough. Knead briefly. Wrap in cling film and leave to chill for 20 minutes.

2 Roll out the pastry on a lightly floured surface and use to line a 24cm loose-bottomed tart tin. Prick the pastry all over and chill for 10 minutes.

3 Preheat the oven to 190°C/375°F/Gas mark 5. Line the pastry case with greaseproof paper and fill with baking beans. Bake for 20 minutes, or until golden and crisp. Remove the paper and beans and leave to cool.

4 For the filling, put the water in a large saucepan. Add the sugar and golden syrup and cook over a low heat until the sugar has dissolved. Increase the heat and let bubble for about 10 minutes until the sauce is a deep caramel colour.

5 Add half of the butter together with the cream and vanilla extract and stand back – it will bubble up. Stir until the mixture is smooth. Pour into the pastry case and chill for 2 hours until set and firm.

6 Melt the chocolate with the remaining butter in a heatproof bowl set over a saucepan of simmering water. Leave to stand for 15 minutes.

7 Pour the chocolate mixture over the top of the tart, spreading it evenly with a spatula. Chill for at least 1 hour to set, then dust with cocoa powder.

Chocolate Tiramisù

Serves 8–10

225g good-quality white chocolate,
  broken into pieces
125ml milk
3 eggs, separated
100g caster sugar
900g mascarpone cheese
125ml Marsala wine
225g amaretti biscuits

For the white chocolate curls
115g good-quality white chocolate

1 Put the chocolate and milk in a heatproof bowl set over a saucepan of simmering water. Heat until the chocolate has melted, then remove from the heat, stir until smooth and leave to cool.

2 Put the egg yolks and sugar in a bowl and whisk until light and frothy. Beat in the cooled chocolate mixture.

3 Spoon the mascarpone into a large mixing bowl and carefully beat in the chocolate mixture. Don't overwork the mascarpone or it will separate.

4 Beat the egg whites in a clean, grease-free bowl until soft peaks form, then fold into the mascarpone mixture. Spoon half the mixture into a serving dish.

5 Pour the Marsala wine into a shallow bowl and dip both sides of the amaretti biscuits in for about 10 seconds, then arrange on top of the mascarpone mixture. Spoon the remaining mascarpone mixture over and leave to chill for at least 3–4 hours.

6 To make the white chocolate curls, melt the chocolate as in step 1, then spread very thinly over a marble slab or work surface. Leave to cool until just hard, then draw the blade of a small sharp knife across the surface, keeping it at a slight angle – the chocolate should roll into curls. Put on greaseproof paper in the refrigerator to set hard, then arrange over the top of the tiramisù.

Cappuccino Truffle Cake

Makes 6–8 slices

1 tablespoon instant coffee powder

150ml boiling water

100g ready-to-eat stoned dried prunes, chopped

4 tablespoons Tia Maria or other coffee liqueur

115g unsalted butter, plus extra for greasing

175g plain chocolate, broken into squares

5 eggs, separated

100g caster sugar

1 teaspoon vanilla extract

1 tablespoon cornflour

Cocoa powder, for dusting

1 Dissolve the coffee powder in the boiling water in a small jug, then pour over the prunes in a bowl. Stir in the liqueur. Leave to soak overnight.

2 Preheat the oven to 160°C/325°F/Gas mark 3. Grease and line a 20cm springform cake tin.

3 Melt the butter and chocolate in a heatproof bowl set over a saucepan of hot water. Remove from the heat.

4 Using a hand-held electric mixer, whisk the egg yolks and sugar together in a separate heatproof bowl set over a saucepan of simmering water, until the mixture is very thick and creamy. Remove from the heat.

5 Drain any excess liquid from the prunes. Stir the vanilla extract, drained prunes and melted chocolate into the creamy mixture and set aside.

6 With clean beaters, whisk the egg whites in a clean, grease-free bowl until stiff. Whisk in the cornflour, then fold this into the chocolate mixture. Pour the mixture evenly into the prepared tin. Bake in the oven for 50 minutes, or until it is springy to the touch.

7 Remove the cake from the oven and leave to cool completely in the tin. Turn the cake out on to a serving plate and dust with cocoa powder. Serve in slices.

Chocolate Amaretto
Cheesecake

Makes 10–12 slices

50g unsalted butter, melted, plus extra
    for greasing
16–18 digestive biscuits
3–4 amaretti biscuits
½ teaspoon almond extract
½ teaspoon ground cinnamon
White chocolate curls, to decorate

For the filling
350g good-quality white chocolate,
    broken into squares
125ml double or whipping cream
675g cream cheese, softened
65g caster sugar
4 eggs
2 tablespoons Amaretto liqueur or
    ½ teaspoon almond extract
½ teaspoon vanilla extract

For the topping
400ml soured cream
50g caster sugar
1 tablespoon Amaretto or
    ½ teaspoon almond extract

1 Preheat the oven to 180°C/350°F/Gas mark 4. Grease a 23cm springform cake tin. Put the biscuits in a food processor and pulse to fine crumbs. Add the butter and flavourings and process to mix. Press the mixture on to the base and sides of the tin. Bake for 5 minutes, then transfer to a wire rack. Reduce the temperature to 150°C/300°F/Gas mark 2.

2 Melt the chocolate and cream in a saucepan over a low heat until smooth. Beat the cheese in a bowl until smooth. Gradually add the sugar, then beat in each egg. Slowly beat in the chocolate mix, Amaretto and vanilla. Spoon over the base. Put on a baking tray and bake for 45-55 minutes until the edge is firm, but the centre is slightly soft. Increase the temperature to 200°C/400°F/Gas mark 6.

3 Beat the topping ingredients together. Spread over the cheesecake and bake for 5-7 minutes. Turn off the oven, but leave the cheesecake inside for 1 hour. Transfer to a wire rack. Run a knife around the edge of the cheesecake, but leave in the tin. Chill overnight. Remove the cheesecake from the tin and decorate with chocolate shavings. Serve in slices.

Chocolate Pudding

Serves 4-6

175g caster sugar
30g cornflour
¼ teaspoon salt
¼ teaspoon ground cinnamon
  (optional)
375ml milk
125ml whipping cream
55g butter, cut into pieces
90g plain chocolate, chopped
1 egg
1 teaspoon vanilla extract

To decorate
Whipped cream
Chocolate shavings

1 Stir together the sugar, cornflour, salt and cinnamon, if using, in a large heavy-based saucepan and gradually whisk in the milk and cream. Add the butter and chocolate and set over a medium heat. Cook until the chocolate melts and the mixture thickens, whisking frequently. Bring to the boil and boil for 1 minute. Remove the pan from the heat.

2 Beat the egg in a small bowl. Stir in a spoonful of the hot chocolate mixture, whisking continuously. Slowly pour the egg into the chocolate mixture, whisking continuously to prevent lumps from forming – the mixture will be very thick. Remove from the heat.

3 Strain the mixture into a large measuring jug, pressing to push the thick mixture through, and stir in the vanilla extract.

4 Pour or spoon the pudding into dessert dishes, custard cups or ramekins and cool. Cover and chill for 2 hours, or overnight. Decorate with whipped cream and a few chocolate shavings on top.

Peppermint Chocolate
Layer Cake

Makes 10–12 slices

75g unsalted butter, plus extra for
  greasing
175g plain chocolate, broken into
  squares
500g caster sugar
3 egg yolks
350ml milk
300g self-raising flour
Pinch of salt
¼ teaspoon bicarbonate of soda
2 teaspoons vanilla extract

For the icing
3 egg whites
400g caster sugar
Pinch of salt
¼ teaspoon cream of tartar
3 tablespoons water
2–3 drops of green food colouring
2–3 drops of peppermint flavouring
50g crushed peppermint sweets

1 Preheat the oven to 180°C/350°F/Gas mark 4. Grease and base-line two 20cm round sandwich cake tins. Melt the chocolate and butter in a heatproof bowl set over a saucepan of simmering water. Leave to cool to room temperature. Stir in the sugar, then add the egg yolks and half of the milk and mix well.

2 Add the flour, salt and bicarbonate of soda and beat for 1 minute using a hand-held electric mixer. Beat in the remaining milk and the vanilla extract. Spoon the mixture into the prepared tins, dividing it evenly, and level the surface. Bake for 25–30 minutes, or until just firm to the touch. Turn out on to a wire rack and leave to cool.

3 For the icing, mix the egg whites, sugar, salt, cream of tartar and water in a heatproof bowl set over a saucepan of simmering water. Whisk for 7 minutes, or until firm peaks form. Remove the bowl from the heat and stir in the food colouring and peppermint flavouring. Sandwich the two cakes together with some icing, then spread the remaining icing evenly over the top and sides of the cake. Decorate with the crushed sweets.

Double Chocolate Chunky

Brownies

Serves 6

225g butter, diced, plus extra for
    greasing
500g plain chocolate
1 teaspoon instant coffee powder
1 tablespoon hot water
3 large eggs
175g caster sugar
1 teaspoon vanilla extract
100g self-raising flour
175g pecan nuts, broken into pieces
Cocoa powder for dusting

Tip
Try not to overcook
the brownies, otherwise
the soft, gooey texture
will be spoiled.

1 Preheat the oven to 190°C/375°F/Gas mark 5. Grease and line a 20 x 30cm cake tin with greaseproof paper.

2 Chop 175g of the chocolate into chunks and set aside. Put the rest in a bowl with the butter and melt slowly over a saucepan of simmering water. Stir until smooth, then leave to cool. Meanwhile, dissolve the coffee in the hot water.

3 Lightly whisk the eggs, coffee, sugar and vanilla extract together in a bowl. Gradually whisk in the chocolate and butter mixture, then fold in the flour, nuts and chocolate chunks. Pour into the prepared tin. Bake for 35–40 minutes, or until firm to the touch.

4 Leave to cool for 5 minutes, then cut into squares. Cool in the tin before removing from the lining paper. Dust with cocoa powder before serving.

Super-quick Bailey's
Chocolate Mousse

Serves 2

50g plain chocolate
125g mascarpone cheese
3 tablespoons Bailey's Irish Cream
    liqueur

1 Break the chocolate into pieces and put in a heatproof bowl set over a saucepan of simmering water. Stir occasionally until the chocolate has melted. Leave to cool slightly.

2 Meanwhile, put the mascarpone and Bailey's in a bowl and beat together until smooth and creamy. Stir in the cooled melted chocolate and chill for at least 30 minutes before serving.

Tip
To make a really indulgent Bailey's sundae, layer spoonfuls of the set mousse and scoops of chocolate and vanilla ice cream in a tall glass, then sprinkle chopped toasted nuts over the top and serve immediately.

Chocolate & Brandy

Truffles

Makes 20–30

225g plain chocolate
1 tablespoon brandy
300ml double cream
25g unsalted butter, cut into cubes
Cocoa powder for dusting

1 Break the chocolate into small pieces and put in a bowl with the brandy.

2 Heat the cream in a saucepan and bring to the boil. Pour over the chocolate, stirring, until the mixture is smooth and glossy. Add the cubes of butter a few at a time, beating until they are incorporated in the mixture. Chill until the mixture is on the point of setting.

3 Beat the mixture with an electric whisk for 3-4 minutes until light and fluffy. Return to the refrigerator to harden completely.

4 Scoop out teaspoons of the truffle mixture, roll into balls and dust in the cocoa powder.

Chocolate Layer Cake

Makes 10 slices

Butter, for greasing
225g plain flour, plus extra for dusting
1½ teaspoons bicarbonate of soda
½ teaspoon baking powder
1 teaspoon salt
350g caster sugar
2 teaspoons vanilla extract
300ml buttermilk
125g white vegetable fat
3 eggs
75g plain chocolate, melted and cooled
Chocolate leaves or curls, to decorate
 (optional)

For the fudgy icing
250ml double cream
450g good-quality plain chocolate,
 chopped
75g unsalted butter, at room
 temperature
1 tablespoon vanilla extract

1 Preheat the oven to 180°C/350°F/Gas mark 4. Grease and flour two 23cm round sandwich cake tins.

2 Sift the flour, bicarbonate of soda, baking powder and salt into a mixing bowl. Add the sugar, vanilla extract, buttermilk, vegetable fat, eggs and cooled melted chocolate. Using a hand-held electric mixer on low speed, begin to beat the mixture slowly until the ingredients are blended, then increase the mixer speed to high and beat for 5 minutes, scraping down the sides of the bowl.

3 Spoon the mixture into the tins, dividing it evenly, then level the surface. Bake for 25 minutes, or until the tops are set. Cool in the tins for 10 minutes, then turn out on to a wire rack and leave to cool completely.

4 For the icing, pour the cream into a saucepan and bring to the boil over a medium-high heat. Remove from the heat and add the chocolate, stirring, until melted and smooth. Beat in the butter and vanilla until well combined. Chill, stirring every 10–15 minutes, until the icing becomes quite thick and spreadable. Remove from the refrigerator and continue to stir occasionally until the icing is thick.

5 Put one cake, top-side up, on a plate and spread with about a quarter of the icing. Put the second cake on top, flat-side up, then spread the top and sides of the cake with the remaining icing. Decorate with chocolate leaves or curls, if liked.

COOL & CREAMY

- Lychee Sorbet
- Blue Lagoon Ice Cream
- Apricot Bavarois
- Raspberry Ripple Shortbread Sandwiches
- Vanilla Ice Cream & Hot Chocolate Sauce
- De Luxe Banana Split
- Mandarin Paradise Parfait
- Creamy Zabaglione
- Lemon Surprise Pudding
- Rose-scented Panacotta
- Cheesecake De Luxe
- Vanilla Cream Millefeuille
- Grasshopper Soufflés
- Raspberry Mousse
- Sweethearts

- Caribbean Coconut Trifle
- Fig & Armagnac Ice Cream
- Fresh Orange Ice Cream Cake
- Gluten-free Fruit Roll
- Coffee Cheesecake with Pecan Sauce
- Strawberry Ice Cream Angel Cake
- Berries Jubilee Sundae
- Ice Cream Pie
- Exotic Iced Delight
- Ice Cream Cake
- Redcurrant Swirl
- Blackcurrant & White Rum Fool

CHAPTER THREE

COOL & CREAMY

Lychee Sorbet

Serves 2

6 tablespoons caster sugar
250ml water
425g can lychees in syrup
1 tablespoon elderflower cordial
1 egg white

Tip

Elderflower cordial adds
a wonderful, scented flavour
to this simple, refreshing sorbet,
but if it's hard to find, lemonade
will have a similar effect.
Whisked egg whites
are added to lighten
the texture.

1 Heat the sugar and water together in a saucepan until the sugar has dissolved. Bring to the boil and simmer for 1 minute. Remove from the heat and leave to cool.

2 Purée the lychees and syrup in a food processor or blender, then pass through a sieve, pressing down well to extract all the juice. Add the elderflower cordial.

3 Pour the mixture into a shallow freezerproof container and freeze for about 2–3 hours until just beginning to hold its shape.

4 Whisk the egg white in a clean, grease-free bowl until soft peaks form, then add to the sorbet. Continue freezing and whisking by hand until it becomes thick and creamy, then freeze until required.

5 Remove from the freezer and put in the refrigerator for 5–10 minutes before serving.

Blue Lagoon Ice Cream

Serves 6

150ml milk
½ vanilla pod
2 egg yolks
5 tablespoons caster sugar
225g blueberries
1 tablespoon water
1 tablespoon white rum
250ml double cream
40g shop-bought meringues

1 Put the milk and vanilla pod in a saucepan and bring to almost boiling point over a low heat. Remove from the heat and take out the vanilla pod. Using a hand-held electric mixer, whisk the egg yolks and 4 tablespoons of the sugar until pale and slightly thickened, then lightly whisk in the milk.

2 Return to a clean heavy-based, non-stick saucepan. Cook over a low heat, stirring continuously, until the mixture thickens to the consistency of double cream and coats the back of a spoon. Cover with cling film and leave to cool. Meanwhile, cook the blueberries with the rest of the sugar and the water for 2 minutes until softened. Leave to cool, then stir in the rum.

3 Whip the cream in a bowl until stiff peaks form and fold into the cold custard. Pour into a shallow freezerproof container and freeze for about 2–3 hours, or until half-frozen. Using a hand-held electric mixer, beat the mixture to break down any ice crystals. Repeat this process at least twice until the ice cream holds its shape. Alternatively, churn in an ice cream maker.

4 Swirl the meringues through the ice cream, followed quickly by the blueberry sauce, to make a marbled pattern. Spoon into a clean freezerproof container and freeze until firm. Remove from the freezer 20–30 minutes before serving.

Tip
If you want to make plain vanilla ice cream, omit the blueberry sauce and meringues, and freeze. Or, if you want to use any other fruit or chocolate sauce, swirl them in, as for the blueberries, at the end.

Apricot Bavarois

Serves 6

450g apricots, halved
2 tablespoons water
1 tablespoon lemon juice
180g sugar
125ml milk
2 tablespoons water
1 tablespoon powdered gelatine
3 eggs, separated
175g double cream
Whipped cream and chocolate curls, to
   decorate

1 Put the apricots in a pan and add the water. Cover and cook gently for 15–20 minutes, until the fruit is soft and pulpy. Remove from the heat and scoop out the pits. Puree the fruit with the lemon juice in a food processor or blender, rub it through a sieve into a bowl, then measure it. There should be 1 cup. If not, add a little fresh orange juice. Stir in 2 tablespoons of the sugar.

2 Put the rest of the sugar in a heatproof bowl and stir the milk, with the sweetened apricot purée. Put the water in a cup and sprinkle the gelatine on top. Leave until spongy. Place the heatproof bowl over a pan of simmering water and stir until the sugar has dissolved, then add the gelatine and continue stirring until that has dissolved, too.

3 In a small bowl, beat the egg yolks with a little of the apricot mixture, then add the mixture to the heatproof bowl. Continue to stir over the heat for about 5 minutes, until the mixture thickens slightly. Leave it to cool, so that it starts to thicken.

4 Whisk the egg whites until soft peaks form. Whip the cream lightly. Fold first the cream and then the egg whites into the apricot mixture, and spoon into a 6-cup dessert bowl. Chill for 3–4 hours, until set. Decorate with whipped cream and chocolate curls.

Raspberry Ripple
Shortbread Sandwiches

Serves 2

4 round shortbread biscuits
2 scoops raspberry ripple ice cream

To decorate (optional)
Fresh berries
Icing sugar

1 Put 2 of the shortbread biscuits on a serving plate and place a scoop of raspberry ripple ice cream on top. Carefully balance the other shortbread cookies on top of the ice cream.

2 Pile fresh summer berries on top of the sandwiches and dust with icing sugar, if liked. Serve at once and eat before the ice cream melts!

Tip
If you fancy something less fruity, why not try plain vanilla ice cream or for something a little sweeter replace the raspberry ripple ice cream with chocolate.

Vanilla Ice Cream

& Hot Chocolate Sauce

Serves 2

300ml milk
1 vanilla pod, split lengthways
   or 1 teaspoon vanilla extract
5 egg yolks
100g caster sugar
300ml double cream

For the hot chocolate sauce
115g plain dark chocolate, chopped
300ml double cream

1 For the ice cream, put the milk and vanilla pod into a saucepan and bring slowly to boiling point, stirring frequently. Remove from the heat and leave to infuse for 15 minutes. Meanwhile, whisk the egg yolks and sugar until thick and pale. Remove the vanilla pod, if using, and pour the milk mixture on to the eggs and sugar, whisking all the time.

2 Return this mixture to a clean saucepan and put over a low heat. Stir continuously with a wooden spoon, until the mixture thickens. Do not allow to boil or the egg will scramble. The custard is ready when the mixture coats the back of a wooden spoon without running off freely. Once the custard has cooled, chill until cold.

3 Whip the cream in a bowl until soft peaks form, then fold into the chilled custard. Pour this mixture into a freezerproof container. Cover and freeze for 2 hours. Remove from the freezer and beat the mixture using an electric or balloon whisk until smooth. Repeat freezing and whisking twice, then freeze until firm. The whisking during freezing prevents large ice crystals forming and ensures that the ice cream is smooth.

4 Put the chocolate into a heatproof bowl. Bring the cream to boiling point in a saucepan, then remove from the heat and leave for a minute to allow it to come off the boil. Pour the cream over the chocolate. Leave to stand for about 1 minute, then stir until smooth. Use immediately as needed.

De Luxe Banana Split

Serves 2

2 scoops each vanilla, chocolate
  and strawberry ice cream
2 ripe bananas
125ml whipping cream, whipped
  and chilled
40g chopped pecan nuts
2 maraschino cherries, drained

For the fudge sauce
225g caster sugar
250ml whipping or double cream
1 tablespoon golden syrup
120g plain chocolate, chopped
2 tablespoons butter, diced
1 teaspoon vanilla extract

For the hot butterscotch sauce
200g light brown sugar
250ml whipping or double cream
2 tablespoons golden syrup
2 tablespoons butter, diced
1 teaspoon rum extract

1 For the fudge sauce, heat the sugar, cream, golden syrup and plain chocolate in a medium, heavy-based saucepan over a medium-high heat, stirring frequently, until the chocolate is melted and the sauce boils. Reduce the heat and stir in the butter and vanilla extract until smooth. Keep warm or leave to cool to room temperature.

2 For the hot butterscotch sauce, put the brown sugar, cream and golden syrup in another saucepan and bring to the boil over a medium-high heat. Boil for 2 minutes, then reduce the heat. Beat in the butter and simmer for a further 2 minutes, or until thickened. Stir in the rum extract and remove from the heat; cover and keep warm.

3 Soften the 3 ice creams to room temperature if necessary, for about 5 minutes. Split each banana in half along its length. Lay two halves in each dish, forming a V-shape. Arrange a scoop of each ice cream along each split banana. Spoon a little of the fudge sauce over the chocolate and strawberry ice creams, and spoon the butterscotch sauce over the vanilla.

4 Pipe or spoon whipped cream over the ice cream, sprinkle with chopped pecans and top with a cherry. Serve the extra sauces separately.

Mandarin Paradise Parfait

Serves 4

300g can mandarin oranges
75g packet orange-flavoured jelly
175g cream cheese, softened

To decorate
Whipped cream
Fresh citrus and passion fruits

1 Drain the mandarins and reserve the juice. Add boiling water to the juice to make 375ml of liquid and dissolve the jelly in it. Hand-beat the cream cheese until smooth and creamy. Slowly add 125ml of the jelly mixture, beating thoroughly to avoid lumps.

2 Cut the mandarins up roughly and add to the cream cheese mixture. Pour half of the remaining jelly mixture into 4 tall glasses and put in the coldest part of the refrigerator to set for 3–4 hours. When ready, pour half the soft cheese mixture into the parfait glasses on top of the set jelly and set, as above. Using the leftover jelly mixture, add the final layer.

3 Decorate with whipped cream. Chop a selection of citrus fruits, such as oranges, grapefruit and clementines, squeezing over them the juice and pips of 1 or 2 passion fruits. Use to decorate the parfaits or serve in a separate bowl for a refreshing and colourful fruit salad accompaniment.

Creamy Zabaglione

Serves 4

4 egg yolks
4 tablespoons caster sugar
100ml Marsala
Grated zest of ½ lemon
150ml double cream, whipped
½ teaspoon vanilla extract
Sponge fingers or biscotti to serve

Tip
Whisking over hot water heats up the mixture and lets the egg yolks cook and thicken the mixture. Take care though – if it overheats, it will separate.

1 Put the egg yolks and sugar into a bowl and whisk over simmering water with an electric hand-held whisk until the mixture is pale yellow, creamy and smooth.

2 Add the Marsala a little at a time, whisking continuously until the mixture is very light and almost thick enough to leave a trail when the beaters are lifted.

3 Remove the bowl from the heat and whisk for a further 5 minutes. Fold in the lemon zest, whipped cream and vanilla extract and serve in glasses with sponge fingers or biscotti to dip in.

Lemon Surprise Pudding

Serves 4

50g butter, softened,
  plus extra for greasing
120g caster sugar
Finely grated zest and juice of 2 large
  lemons
2 eggs, separated
50g self-raising flour
175ml milk
Cream, to serve

1 Preheat the oven to 180°C/350°F/Gas mark 4. Grease a 900ml pudding basin or baking dish and set aside.

2 Beat the butter, sugar and lemon zest together until well mixed. Next beat in the egg yolks, a little at a time. Fold in the flour, alternating with the milk and lemon juice. Finally, whisk the egg whites in a clean, grease-free bowl and fold them into the mixture. At this stage, the mixture will look curdled, but this is to be expected.

3 Pour the mixture into the prepared pudding basin or baking dish and bake in the centre of the oven for 40–45 minutes until golden brown and risen. Serve hot with pouring cream.

Rose-scented Panacotta

Serves 2

2 leaves gelatine
3 tablespoons milk
480ml whipping cream
2 tablespoons caster sugar
1 tablespoon rosewater
Fresh rose petals, to decorate

1 Soak the gelatine in the milk until soft. Put the cream, sugar and rosewater in a small saucepan and heat gently until almost boiling. Remove from the heat and leave to cool. Add the milk from the gelatine and, once cooled, add the gelatine itself. Stir until completely dissolved.

2 Pour the mixture into two 180ml dariole moulds or pudding basins. Cover and refrigerate overnight. Unmould, decorate with rose petals and serve.

Tip

If the panacotta is proving difficult to remove from the moulds, briefly dip the base of the moulds in boiling water.

Cheesecake De Luxe

Serves 4

For the base
225g fine digestive crumbed biscuits
3 tablespoons caster sugar
1 teaspoon ground cinnamon
½ teaspoon freshly grated nutmeg
85g butter

For the filling
50g butter
100g caster sugar
⅛ teaspoon salt
1 tablespoon grated lemon zest
3 large eggs, separated
Juice of 1 lemon
½ teaspoon vanilla extract
Two 225g tubs cream cheese
225ml soured cream

1 Preheat the oven to 150°C/300°F/Gas mark 2. To make the base, combine the biscuit crumbs with the sugar, cinnamon and nutmeg. Melt the butter, blend it into the crumb mixture, and pack firmly against the base and sides of a 23cm springform cake tin or ovenproof glass dish. Leave to chill until required.

2 For the filling, cream the butter, sugar, salt and lemon zest together in a bowl. Slowly beat the egg yolks into the creamed mixture. Add the lemon juice, vanilla extract, cream cheese and soured cream. Whisk the egg whites in a clean, grease-free bowl until soft peaks form. Fold into the other ingredients and ladle onto the base.

3 Bake the cheesecake for 1–1¼ hours until firm. Leave to cool in the tin, then remove from the tin and onto a serving plate. Chill for several hours in the refrigerator before serving.

Vanilla Cream Millefeuille

Serves 8

350g ready-made puff pastry
25g icing sugar

For the filling
500ml milk
1 vanilla pod
1 teaspoon vanilla extract
5 egg yolks
120g caster sugar
1 tablespoon plain flour
1 tablespoon cornflour
250ml double cream
450g strawberries, thinly sliced

1 Roll out the pastry to a rectangle 30 x 22cm. Halve lengthways and put on a non-stick baking sheet. Sift the icing sugar over one half of the pastry and score into diamond shapes using the tip of a sharp knife. Chill for 30 minutes.

2 Preheat the oven to 200°C/400°F/Gas mark 6. Bake the pastry halves for 15–20 minutes until puffed and golden. Cool, then split the unsugared pastry horizontally, discarding the top. Split the sugared half horizontally, reserving both pieces.

3 Put the milk, vanilla pod and vanilla extract into a large saucepan and slowly bring to the boil. Whisk the egg yolks with the sugar, flour and cornflour. Add the hot milk and mix well. Remove the vanilla pod and scrape out the seeds, stirring them into the custard. Cook, stirring, for 4–5 minutes until the custard has thickened. Cover with cling film and leave to cool completely.

4 Whip the cream until soft peaks form and fold into the cooled custard. Spread half of the custard over the unsugared piece of pastry and cover with half the strawberries.

5 Put the base of the split sugared piece over the fruit and press down. Spread the remaining custard over and top with the rest of the strawberries. Put the sugared pastry on top.

Grasshopper Soufflés

Serves 2

2 envelopes unflavoured gelatine
500ml water
200g caster sugar
4 medium eggs, separated
225g tub cream cheese, softened
60ml crème de menthe
225ml double cream, whipped

To decorate
Candied flowers
Fresh mint leaves

1 Put the gelatine with 125ml water in a saucepan. Add the remaining water when it is softened. Stir over a low heat until dissolved. Remove from the heat and blend in 150g sugar and lightly beaten egg yolks. Return to the heat and simmer for 2-3 minutes. Remove from the heat and set to one side.

2 Put the softened cream cheese in a large mixing bowl. Whisk with an electric mixer. Gradually add the cooked mixture to the cream cheese, mixing until well blended. Stir in the crème de menthe. Chill for 15 minutes until slightly thickened.

3 Whisk the egg whites in a clean bowl until soft peaks form. Gradually add the remaining 50g sugar, beating until stiff peaks form. Fold into the chilled cream cheese mixture. Fold in the whipped cream (reserve a small amount for decoration, if desired).

4 Wrap 7.5cm collars of aluminium foil around the rims of the four soufflé dishes, so that the foil extends beyond the rims of the dishes, and secure with tape. Pour the mixture into the dishes and chill for 1 hour until firm. Remove the foil collars before serving. Decorate with candied flowers and mint leaves.

Raspberry Mousse

Serves 6

2 pints fresh raspberries
2 tablespoons icing sugar
2 tablespoons lemon juice
60ml water
1 tablespoon powdered gelatine
2 eggs, plus 1 egg yolk
6 tablespoons sugar
250g double cream
Whipped cream, to decorate

1 Set aside a few raspberries for decoration. Put the rest in a food processor or blender and add the icing sugar and lemon juice. Process to a purée, then remove the seeds by pressing the purée through a sieve placed over a bowl.

2 Pour the water into a metal measuring cup and sprinkle with the gelatine on top. When it is spongy, set the cup over simmering water until the gelatine melts.

3 Meanwhile, place the eggs, egg yolk, and sugar in the top of a double boiler. Whisk over simmering water until the mixture is very thick, then remove from the heat and gently fold in the gelatine mixture, with 250g of the raspberry purée. Save the remaining purée for a sauce.

4 Whip the double cream to soft peaks and fold it into the mixture. Spoon into a glass bowl and chill for 3-4 hours, until set.

5 Decorate with whipped cream and the reserved raspberries. Taste the raspberry sauce and add a little extra sugar if you like. Serve with the mousse.

Sweethearts

Serves 2

115g good-quality white chocolate,
broken into pieces
1 tablespoon golden syrup
1 tablespoon brandy
150ml double cream
2 fresh strawberries, to serve

For the strawberry sauce
110g strawberries, hulled
1 tablespoon icing sugar, plus extra for
dusting

1 Put the chocolate in a heatproof bowl. Add the golden syrup and brandy. Put the bowl over a saucepan of gently simmering water and melt the chocolate, stirring the mixture occasionally.

2 Remove from the heat and leave to cool slightly. Whip the cream in a bowl until soft peaks form and carefully fold it into the chocolate mixture. Spoon into two 125ml heart-shaped moulds and leave to set in the refrigerator for at least 2 hours.

3 For the sauce, put the strawberries and icing sugar in a food processor or blender and process until puréed. Press through a sieve to remove the seeds.

4 Run a knife gently around the edge of each chocolate heart, then carefully invert the moulds and transfer on to 2 dessert plates. Drizzle the sauce around the hearts and decorate with the fresh strawberries. Dust with extra icing sugar.

Caribbean Coconut Trifle

Serves 2

350g sweet pineapple flesh
300ml double cream
4 tablespoons coconut milk
200ml crème fraîche
4 tablespoons icing sugar
2 papaya, peeled, seeded and chopped
2 mangoes, peeled, stoned and
    chopped
Juice of 1 lime
Toasted flaked coconut, to decorate

Tip

As an extra treat, add a splash of rum to the mix to give it that extra kick.

1 Cut the pineapple into large chunks, put in a food processor or blender and process briefly until chopped. Tip into a sieve and reserve the juice for later.

2 Whip the cream in a large bowl until soft peaks form, then lightly fold in the coconut milk, crème fraîche and icing sugar.

3 Fold the drained pineapple into the cream mixture. Put the papaya and mango in a large serving bowl and pour over the lime juice and 4 tablespoons of the drained pineapple juice.

4 Spoon the pineapple cream on top of the fruit and scatter over the toasted coconut flakes.

Fig & Armagnac Ice Cream

Serves 4–6

450g ripe fresh figs, cut into quarters
3 tablespoons Armagnac or brandy
300ml milk
4 egg yolks
175g caster sugar
300ml double cream
1 teaspoon vanilla extract
Fresh figs, cut into slices, to serve

1 Put the figs in a food processor or blender with the Armagnac or brandy and process to a purée. Meanwhile, heat the milk in a saucepan over a low heat until almost boiling.

2 Whisk the egg yolks with 120g of the sugar with a hand-held electric mixer until pale and slightly thickened, then lightly whisk in the hot milk.

3 Return to a clean, non-stick saucepan. Cook over a low heat, stirring continuously, until the mixture thickens to the consistency of double cream and coats the back of a spoon. Cover with cling film and leave to cool.

4 Lightly whip the cream in a bowl until soft peaks form, then fold it into the cold custard with the puréed figs and vanilla extract. Taste the mixture and add the remaining sugar, if needed.

5 Pour into a shallow freezerproof container and freeze until half-frozen, about 2–3 hours, then beat with a hand-held electric mixer to break down any ice crystals. Repeat this process at least twice more until the ice cream holds its shape. Alternatively, churn in an ice cream maker.

6 Remove from the freezer 20–30 minutes before serving. Serve in scoops with slices of fresh figs.

Tip

The more ripe and flavourful the figs that you use, the better this sophisticated ice cream will taste.

Fresh Orange
Ice Cream Cake

Serves 8

4 oranges
5 eggs, separated
275g caster sugar
500ml double cream
115g sponge fingers
75ml Grand Marnier

1 Line a 23cm springform cake tin with cling film.

2 Carefully cut the peel off one orange, removing as much of the white pith as possible. Cut between the separating membranes and lift out the segments. Arrange around the base of the cake tin.

3 Grate the zest of the remaining 3 oranges and set aside. Squeeze the juice from the 3 oranges into a saucepan. Bring to the boil and cook until reduced by half.

4 Put the egg yolks in a large bowl with 225g of the sugar and beat with a hand-held electric mixer until thick and frothy. Whisk in the reduced orange juice and grated zest and leave to cool. Lightly whip the cream in another bowl, then fold into the orange custard.

5 Whisk the egg whites in a clean, grease-free bowl until stiff peaks form and whisk in the remaining sugar, a tablespoon at a time. Next, fold the mixture into the orange cream.

6 Pour half the mixture over the orange segments in the cake tin. Dip the sponge fingers into the Grand Marnier and arrange in a layer across the orange cream. Spoon the remaining mixture over, cover, and freeze for 7–8 hours.

7 Invert the frozen orange cake on to a serving plate and put in the refrigerator for 30 minutes before serving.

Gluten-free Fruit Roll

Makes 8–10 slices

Butter, for greasing
4 eggs, separated
125g icing sugar, plus extra for dusting
1 tablespoon orange flower water
50g rice flour
50g potato flour
1 teaspoon gluten-free baking powder

For the filling
300ml natural yoghurt
½ large mango, peeled, stoned and chopped
¼ small papaya, peeled, seeded and chopped
1 passion fruit

To decorate
Fresh mango slices
1 passion fruit, cut in half

1 Preheat the oven to 190°C/375°F/Gas mark 5. Grease and line a 32 x 22cm Swiss roll tin, then grease the lining paper. For the cake, put the egg whites in a clean bowl and whisk until soft peaks form. Sift half of the icing sugar over the top and whisk in. Whisk the egg yolks with the remaining icing sugar in another bowl until the mixture is pale and very thick. Stir in the orange flower water. Sift the flours and baking powder over the top and fold in. Using a metal spoon, fold in the whisked egg whites mixture, one-third at a time.

2 Spoon the mixture into the tin, spreading it evenly. Bake in the oven for about 12–15 minutes, or until springy to the touch. Sprinkle a little extra sifted icing sugar over a large sheet of non-stick baking paper and turn out the sponge cake on to the paper. Remove the lining paper, trim off any firm edges, then loosely roll up the cake with the paper inside and leave to cool on a wire rack. For the filling, carefully unroll the cake and spread the yoghurt evenly over the cake. Scatter over the chopped mango and papaya. Halve the passion fruit and spoon the juice and seeds over the fruit.

3 Carefully roll up the cake, put it on a serving plate and dust with extra sifted icing sugar. Decorate with slices of mango and the juice and seeds of the passion fruit. Serve in slices.

Coffee Cheesecake

With Pecan Sauce

Serves 6

200g digestive biscuits
55g unsalted butter, melted
600g cream cheese
200g soft brown sugar
1 teaspoon vanilla extract
3 eggs
2 tablespoons very strong
    brewed coffee

For the sauce
55g unsalted butter
75g soft brown sugar
250ml double cream
1 teaspoon vanilla extract
75g pecans, toasted and
    finely chopped

1 Crush the biscuits into fine crumbs and stir in the melted butter. Press into the base of a 20cm springform cake tin and chill for 20 minutes.

2 Preheat the oven to 180°C/350°F/Gas mark 4. Beat the cream cheese with the sugar and vanilla extract. Add the eggs and beat until smooth. Stir in the coffee, then spoon into the cake tin.

3 Put the cake tin in a roasting tin half-full of boiling water and cook in the oven for 55 minutes. Turn off the heat and let the cheesecake cool in the oven for 1 hour, then transfer to the refrigerator before serving.

4 For the sauce, melt the butter in a small saucepan and add the sugar, cream and vanilla extract. Simmer for 10 minutes, then stir in the pecans. Serve warm with the cheesecake.

Tip
Avoid overbeating the mixture. Overbeating incorporates additional air and tends to cause cracking on the surface of the cheesecake.

Strawberry Ice Cream

Angel Cake

Serves 6–8

50g plain flour
2 tablespoons cornflour
200g caster sugar
7 large egg whites
¾ teaspoon cream of tartar
Pinch of salt
1½ teaspoons vanilla extract
Fresh strawberries, to serve

For the filling
4 tablespoons strawberry jam
500ml strawberry ice cream

1 Preheat the oven to 180°C/350°F/Gas mark 4. Sift the flour and cornflour together. Add 75g caster sugar and sift together twice.

2 Whisk the egg whites in a clean, grease-free bowl until foamy. Add the cream of tartar and salt and continue whisking until they are stiff.

3 Whisk the remaining sugar into the egg whites a spoonful at a time until stiff peaks form and are glossy. Whisk in the vanilla extract.

4 Fold in the flour in 3 batches, then spoon into a 23cm springform tube tin. The mixture should come up to the top of the tin. Level the top and bake for 45-50 minutes, or until lightly golden on top and spongy to the touch. Remove from the oven and invert on to a wire rack. Leave in the tin until cool.

5 Remove the cake from the tin and cool. Wash and dry the tin and line with non-stick baking paper. Cut the cake horizontally and return the base to the tin. Spread the jam over the base and top with ice cream, spreading over evenly. Top with the other half and press down lightly. Freeze until firm. Serve topped with fresh strawberries.

Berries Jubilee Sundae

Serves 2

2 teaspoons unflavoured gelatine
60ml cold water
175ml milk
1 vanilla pod
150g sugar
⅛ teaspoon salt
750ml double cream, whipped
Nuts, fudge pieces, maraschino
  cherries and chocolate novelties to
  decorate

For the berry cream
500g hulled strawberries,
  raspberries or blueberrries
200g caster sugar
2 tablespoons unflavoured gelatine
2 tablespoons cold water
3 tablespoons boiling water
1 tablespoon lemon juice
500ml double cream, whipped

For the jubilee sauce
290g fresh or frozen stoned sweet
  cherries, at room temperature
60ml brandy, slightly warmed
2 tablespoons kirsch

1 For the ice cream, soak the gelatine in 60ml cold water for 10 minutes. Boil milk with the vanilla pod in a heavy-based saucepan and leave for 20 minutes. Stir in the sugar and salt, then add the gelatine. Pour into a container and cool, then freeze for 1–2 hours, or until ice crystals start to form and it is firm all the way through. Whisk the mixture until thickened but not stiff, then fold in the cream. Freeze overnight.

2 For the berry cream, put the berries and sugar in a bowl and crush. Leave to stand for 1 hour. Dissolve the gelatine in the 2 tablespoons cold water, then add the 3 tablespoons boiling water. Stir in the crushed berries and the lemon juice. When cool, fold in the whipped cream. Pour into a wet mould and chill overnight.

3 For the jubilee sauce, heat the cherries in a saucepan. Add the brandy and set on fire. When the flames have died down, add the kirsch. Layer the sauce, berry cream and ice cream into sundae glasses and decorate with nuts, fudge, cherries and chocolate novelties.

Ice Cream Pie

Serves 6-8

175g chocolate chip cookies, crushed
85g unsalted butter, melted

For the filling
750ml vanilla ice cream, slightly
   softened
750ml chocolate ice cream, slightly
   softened

For the sauce
150g milk chocolate, broken into
   pieces
25g unsalted butter
30g golden syrup
3 tablespoons water
25g finely chopped hazelnuts

1 Mix the crushed cookies with the melted butter and press the mixture into the base and halfway up the sides of a 20cm springform cake tin. Chill for 20 minutes, or until firm.

2 Pile alternate scoops of vanilla and chocolate ice cream over the cookie base, leaving the top quite rough. Freeze for at least 1 hour, or until the ice cream is firm.

3 Meanwhile, make the sauce. Put the chocolate, butter and golden syrup in a heatproof bowl with the water and melt over a saucepan of gently simmering water. Stir until smooth, then remove from the heat and leave to cool.

4 Preheat the grill. Toast the finely chopped hazelnuts under the grill for 2-3 minutes, or until dark golden.

5 Remove the pie from the tin. Pour the sauce over the ice cream and scatter with the toasted hazelnuts. Freeze until ready to serve, or serve immediately.

Exotic Iced Delight

Serves 2–4

1 large mango, peeled and stoned
300ml custard sauce (see tip) or carton
  fresh custard
300ml double cream

To decorate
Chopped toasted pecans
Maple syrup

1 Put the mango flesh in a food processor and process to a purée. Pour the custard into a bowl and stir in the mango purée. Whip the cream until soft peaks form and fold into the custard mixture.

2 Pour the mixture into a shallow freezerproof container and cover with an airtight lid. Freeze for 1 hour, then beat with a fork to break up any large ice crystals.

3 Return the ice cream to the freezer for 2 hours, then beat again. Finally, return to the freezer for 4 hours, or until frozen. Scoop the ice cream into glasses, sprinkle with toasted pecans and drizzle with maple syrup before serving.

Tip

To make the custard sauce:
Mix 2 teaspoons cornflour with 2 tablespoons single cream in a cup. Beat 2 egg yolks in a bowl until pale, then stir in the cornflour mix. Heat 250ml single cream with 4 tablespoons sugar in a saucepan. When hot, pour half the hot cream on to the egg mixture, stirring, then add the mixture to the remaining hot cream in the pan. Cook for 5 minutes until thick, then stir in ½ teaspoon vanilla extract. Cover and cool.

Ice Cream Cake

Serves 10–12

300g caster sugar
120g cake flour
8 medium egg whites, at room
    temperature
1¼ teaspoons cream of tartar
Pinch of salt
1 teaspoon almond extract
½ teaspoon vanilla extract
6–8 maraschino cherries (optional)
Icing sugar, for dusting

For the filling
Scoops of ice cream, preferably
    vanilla, enough to fill centre core
450g can yellow peaches, drained
Fresh strawberries and raspberries

For the Melba sauce
150g caster sugar
125ml water
450g fresh strawberries or raspberries,
    puréed and chilled

1 Preheat the oven to 180°C/350°F/Gas mark 4. Sift the sugar twice. Sift the flour 4 times in a separate bowl. Set both aside. Beat the egg whites in a clean, grease-free bowl until frothy. Add the cream of tartar and salt and continue to whisk until soft peaks forms. Sprinkle 2 tablespoons sugar over the egg white peaks and beat until blended. Repeat the process until the sugar is used up. Beat in the almond and vanilla extracts. With a rubber spatula, fold in the flour, 35g at a time. If using, cut the cherries into quarters and fold into the mixture.

2 Spoon the mixture into an ungreased 24cm fluted ring mould. Cut through it with a knife to get rid of any air bubbles and level off. Bake in the centre of the oven for 40–60 minutes until the top turns light brown.

3 Put all the ingredients for the Melba sauce in a saucepan and bring to the boil, stirring occasionally until the sugar dissolves. Leave to cool.

4 Remove the cake from the oven, invert on to a wire rack and leave to cool in the mould for 1 hour. Run a sharp knife around the edges of the mould to loosen the cake before inverting on to a serving plate. Fill the centre with ice cream and fruit. Drizzle over the Melba sauce and dust with icing sugar.

Redcurrant Swirl

Serves 4–6

225g granulated sugar
600ml water
150ml rosé or red wine
550g redcurrants, stripped from
their stalks
3 tablespoons arrowroot mixed to a
paste with 3 tablespoons water
4–6 tablespoons soured cream

1 Put the sugar and water in a saucepan. Heat, stirring, until the sugar dissolves, then bring to the boil and cook, without stirring for 2–3 minutes. Stir in the wine.

2 Add the redcurrants to the wine syrup, reduce the heat, and poach them for about 10 minutes until just tender.

3 Stir in the arrowroot paste. Bring to the boil, stirring continuously until the mixture thickens. Leave to cool, then chill for several hours. Serve in individual glass dishes, swirling 1 tablespoon of soured cream on the surface of each portion.

Tip

Arrowroot is preferable to cornflour for thickening this particular sauce as it gives a clear, rather than a cloudy, result.

Blackcurrant
& White Rum Fool

Serves 4

450g fresh or frozen blackcurrants
50g caster sugar
2 tablespoons fresh orange juice
2 tablespoons white rum
300ml double cream, lightly whipped

For the custard
150ml full-fat milk
½ vanilla pod
2 egg yolks
50g caster sugar

1 Make a fruit purée by cooking the blackcurrants, caster sugar and orange juice in a covered saucepan until very soft for 5 minutes. Leave to cool, then purée in a food processor or blender. Push the juice and pulp through a sieve. Stir in the white rum and set aside.

2 For the custard, heat the milk and vanilla pod together over a low heat until the milk almost boils. Remove from the heat and remove the vanilla pod. Whisk the egg yolks and sugar together until pale and slightly thickened, then whisk in the milk.

3 Return the mixture to a heavy-based non-stick saucepan. Cook over a low heat, stirring continuously, until the mixture thickens to the consistency of double cream. Cover the surface with cling film and leave to cool.

4 Stir the blackcurrant purée into the custard and then gently fold in the whipped cream. Stir gently until it thickens slightly, then spoon into glasses and chill before serving.

PIES & TARTS

- Raisin Cheese Pie
- Chess Pie
- Coffee & Walnut Pie
- Georgia Pecan Pie
- Freeform Strawberry Rhubarb Pie
- Strawberry & Custard Tartlets
- Peanut Butter Pie
- Banana Tarte Tatin
- Bourbon Pie
- Fig & Ricotta Tart
- Tarte Fine aux Pommes
- Honey & Mixed Nut Tart
- Orange Chiffon Pie
- Banana Cream Pie

- Marlborough Pie
- Freeform Spiced Plum Pie
- Caramel Cream Pie
- Blacksmith Pie
- Pear Tart with Walnut & Star Anise
- Chocolate Chip & Peanut Butter Pie
- Frangipani Cream Pie
- Figgy Meringue Tarts
- Apple & Cinnamon Pie
- Black Bottom Cream Pie
- Raspberry & Coconut Pie
- Lemon Chiffon Pie
- Cherry Pie

CHAPTER FOUR

PIES & TARTS

Raisin Cheese Pie

Serves 8

75g plain flour, plus extra for dusting
75g self-raising flour
90g butter, diced
2 tablespoons cold water

For the filling
75g seedless raisins
2 tablespoons dark rum or orange
  juice
225g curd or ricotta cheese
2 eggs, separated
50g sugar
1 teaspoon vanilla extract
160ml double cream

To decorate
Fresh mint leaves
Fresh raspberries

1 Sift the flours into a mixing bowl. Add the butter and rub it in until the mixture resembles breadcrumbs. Sprinkle the water over the dry ingredients and mix to a firm dough. Knead briefly, then wrap in cling film and chill for 30 minutes.

2 For the filling, put the raisins in a small bowl with the rum or orange juice and leave to soak.

3 Preheat the oven to 200°C/400°F/Gas mark 6. Roll out the pastry on a lightly floured surface and use to line a 23cm plain tart tin. Prick the base all over, then chill for 15 minutes.

4 Line the pastry case with non-stick baking paper and baking beans. Bake blind for 10 minutes. Remove the paper and beans and bake for 5 minutes. Reduce the temperature to 150°C/300°F/Gas mark 2. Beat the cheese until soft, then stir in the raisins. Beat the egg yolks, sugar and vanilla extract in another bowl until pale. Add the cream and continue beating until stiff. Fold into the raisin mixture.

5 Beat the egg whites in a clean bowl until stiff, then fold into the cheese mixture. Spoon into the pastry case and bake for 45 minutes–1 hour, or until just set. Turn off the heat and cool in the oven for 15 minutes. Cool in the tin, then chill overnight. Decorate with mint leaves and raspberries.

Chess Pie

Serves 8

175g plain flour, plus extra for dusting
Pinch of salt
75g chilled butter, diced
2 tablespoons cold water
1–2 teaspoons icing sugar, for dusting

For the filling

115g butter, softened
225g caster sugar
Finely grated zest of ½ lemon
Pinch of salt
3 egg yolks
1 tablespoon lemon juice

1 Sift the flour and salt into a mixing bowl. Add the butter and rub it in until the mixture resembles breadcrumbs. Sprinkle over the water and mix to a firm dough. Knead briefly, wrap in cling film and chill for 30 minutes.

2 Put a baking sheet in the oven and preheat to 200°C/400°F/Gas mark 6. Roll out the pastry on a floured surface and use to line a shallow 23cm tart tin. Prick the base all over with a fork, then chill for 10 minutes.

3 Line the pastry case with non-stick baking paper and fill with baking beans. Bake for 15 minutes. Remove the paper and beans, then bake for a further 5 minutes. Reduce the temperature to 160°C/325°F/Gas mark 3.

4 Cream the butter, sugar, lemon zest and salt together in a bowl until light and fluffy. Beat in the egg yolks, one at a time, then stir in the lemon juice.

5 Spoon the filling into the pastry case and roughly spread it out. Bake for a further 25-30 minutes, or until lightly set.

6 Leave the pie to settle for 10 minutes before removing from the tin. Dust with icing sugar.

Coffee & Walnut Pie

Serves 4–6

150g plain flour, plus extra for dusting
Pinch of salt
75g butter, diced
2–3 tablespoons cold water
Whipped cream or ice cream, to serve

For the filling
180ml maple syrup
1 tablespoon instant coffee granules
1 tablespoon boiling water
25g butter, softened
130g golden brown sugar
3 eggs, beaten
1 teaspoon vanilla extract
75g walnut halves

1 Sift the flour and salt into a mixing bowl. Add the butter and rub it in until the mixture resembles fine breadcrumbs. Add 2 tablespoons cold water and, using a spatula, start to bring the dough together, adding a little more water, if necessary. Knead briefly, then wrap in cling film and chill for 20 minutes.

2 Roll out the pastry on a lightly floured surface to a rough round at least 5cm in diameter larger than a loose-bottomed 23cm fluted tart tin. Gently roll the pastry on to the rolling pin, then unroll it over the pan to cover. Press the pastry into the edge of the tin, removing any overhanging pastry with a knife. Prick the base. Chill for 20 minutes.

3 Put a baking sheet in the oven and preheat to 200°C/400°F/Gas mark 6. Line the pastry case with non-stick baking paper and fill with baking beans. Bake blind for 12 minutes. Remove the paper and beans and bake for a further 10 minutes, or until golden. Leave to cool. Reduce the oven temperature to 180°C/350°F/Gas mark 4.

4 For the filling, put the maple syrup in a saucepan and heat until almost boiling. Mix the coffee granules with the boiling water, stirring until they have completely dissolved. Stir this mixture into the maple syrup. Leave until just warm.

5 Combine the butter and sugar, and gradually beat in the eggs. Add the cooled maple syrup mixture with the vanilla extract, and stir well.

6 Arrange the walnut halves in the base of the pastry case, then carefully pour in the filling. Transfer to the oven and bake for 30–35 minutes, or until browned and firm. Leave to cool for about 10 minutes. Serve with whipped cream or ice cream.

Georgia Pecan Pie

Serves 8–10

175g plain flour, plus extra for dusting
75g cream cheese
120g butter
2 tablespoons granulated sugar
Whipped cream or ice cream, to serve

For the filling
350g–400g pecan nut halves
3 eggs, lightly beaten
200g dark brown sugar
125ml golden syrup
Grated zest and juice of ½ lemon
55g butter, melted and cooled
2 teaspoons vanilla extract

1 Sift the flour into a mixing bowl. Add the cream cheese, butter and sugar and rub it in until the mixture resembles fine breadcrumbs. Form the dough into a ball, then flatten and wrap in cling film. Chill 1 hour.

2 Roll the dough out on a lightly floured surface and carefully line the base and sides of a 23cm tart tin. Crimp the edge and chill.

3 Preheat the oven to 180°C/350°F/Gas mark 4. Pick out 110g perfect pecan halves and set aside. Coarsely chop the remaining nuts.

4 For the filling, whisk the eggs and brown sugar together in a bowl until light and foamy. Beat in the golden syrup, lemon zest and juice, melted butter and vanilla extract. Stir in the chopped pecans and pour into the tart tin.

5 Set the pie on a baking sheet and carefully arrange the reserved pecan halves in concentric circles on top of the mixture.

6 Bake for 45 minutes until the filling has risen and set and the pecans have coloured. Transfer to a wire rack to cool to room temperature. Serve with whipped cream or ice cream.

Freeform Strawberry
Rhubarb Pie

Serves 4–6

120g plain flour, plus extra for dusting
Pinch of salt
75g butter diced
60g ground almonds
55g caster sugar
3–4 tablespoons cold water

For the filling
450g rhubarb, cut into chunks
75–120g sugar, to taste
1 vanilla pod
2 strips lemon zest
2 teaspoons cornflour or arrowroot
350g strawberries, hulled and
   halved if large
2 teaspoons coarse sugar

1 Sift the flour and salt into a mixing bowl. Add the butter and rub it in with the ground almonds and sugar until the mixture resembles coarse breadcrumbs. Add enough cold water to form a dough. Knead briefly, then wrap in cling film and chill for at least 20 minutes.

2 For the filling, put the rhubarb, 75g sugar, vanilla pod and lemon zest into a saucepan over a low heat. Cook, stirring frequently, for 8-10 minutes until the rhubarb is tender and quite juicy but still holding its shape. Taste for sweetness and add the remaining sugar if necessary.

3 Mix the cornflour and a little water together until smooth. Stir in the rhubarb, then return to a gentle simmer. Cook for 1-2 minutes until thickened. Remove from the heat and stir in the strawberries. Leave to cool. Remove the vanilla pod and lemon zest.

4 Preheat the oven to 200°C/400°F/Gas mark 6. Roll the pastry out on a lightly floured surface to a large round about 38cm in diameter. Transfer to a large, non-stick baking sheet. Spoon the cold rhubarb mixture into the centre of the pastry and gather the pastry around the filling, leaving an open top. Brush the pastry with a little cold water and sprinkle with the coarse sugar.

5 Bake in the centre of the oven for about 20–25 minutes. Leave to cool, then cut into wedges and serve.

Tip

A freeform pie is a great way to toss together something tasty when you don't have much time to make dessert. For fruit such as rhubarb, pears and apples it's best to heat them over a low heat first to soften them up. With softer fruit such as nectarines, peaches and bananas they will not need cooking as they will soften in the time it takes for the pie to bake. Just toss them with a little sugar.

Strawberry & Custard
Tartlets

Makes 2

100g plain flour, plus extra
  for dusting
3 tablespoons icing sugar
55g butter
About 1 tablespoon water

For the filling
150ml milk
1 egg yolk
2 tablespoons caster sugar
2 tablespoons plain flour

For the topping
6–8 strawberries, hulled
1 tablespoon strawberry jam

1 Sift the flour and icing sugar into a mixing bowl. Add the butter and rub it in until the mixture resembles breadcrumbs. Sprinkle over the water and mix to a firm dough. Knead briefly, wrap in cling film and chill for 30 minutes.

2 Roll out the dough on a lightly floured surface and use to line two 8cm tartlet tins. Prick the bases all over with a fork and chill for 10 minutes.

3 Preheat the oven to 200°C/400°F/Gas mark 6. Line the pastry cases with non-stick baking paper and fill with baking beans. Bake for 15–20 minutes. Remove the paper and beans and bake for 5 minutes until pale golden. Leave to cool.

4 For the custard filling, beat the milk, egg yolk, sugar and flour in a bowl. Pour into a small saucepan and cook, stirring continuously until the mixture comes to the boil. Beat the custard until smooth, then simmer for 2 minutes. Leave to cool, then spoon into the tartlet cases.

5 Arrange the strawberries on top of the custard. Warm the jam and brush it over the top. Leave to set for a few minutes before serving.

Peanut Butter Pie

Serves 8

3 eggs
250ml golden syrup
120g caster sugar
120g creamy peanut butter
½ teaspoon vanilla
75g salted peanuts, coarsely chopped

For the topping
375ml double cream
2 tablespoons granulated sugar
½ teaspoon vanilla extract
Pie shell, never-fail or extra flaky

1 Chill an unbaked pie shell.

2 Beat the eggs and add the golden syrup, sugar, peanut butter, and vanilla. Beat until smooth. Blend the salted peanuts into the mixture. Pour the filling into the chilled, unbaked pie shell and bake for 15 minutes at 200°C/400°F/Gas mark 6. Turn down the heat to 180°C/350°F/Gas mark 4 and bake for an additional 30–35 minutes. Let cool.

3 Whip the double cream with the sugar and vanilla. Spread over the pie after it has cooled and serve.

Banana Tarte Tatin

Serves 4–6

55g butter, plus extra for greasing
5 bananas
120g caster sugar
2 tablespoons boiling water
2 pinches of ground cinnamon
250g ready-made puff pastry
Plain flour, for dusting
Whipped cream, to serve

Tip

The riper the bananas the better the taste. Try not to buy ones that are too ripe otherwise the dessert may go mushy.

1 Preheat the oven to 200°C/400°F/Gas mark 6. Grease a non-stick 23cm cake tin.

2 Slice the bananas into 1cm rounds. Melt the butter with the sugar in a large frying pan. Add the water and stir over a high heat until the sugar has dissolved and the water is a warm caramel colour. Add the bananas to the frying pan and cook for 1–2 minutes. Sprinkle the cinnamon over the bananas, then spoon them into the greased tin.

3 Roll the pastry out on a lightly floured surface to a round about 2.5cm bigger than the cake tin. Drape it over the bananas and tuck the edges in. Bake for 20 minutes until the pastry is puffed and golden. Put a large serving plate over the tin and turn it upside down so the pastry is on the bottom. Remove the cake tin and leave for 5 minutes before serving with whipped cream.

Bourbon Pie

Serves 8–10

175g plain flour, plus extra for dusting
Pinch of salt
90g chilled butter, diced
2 tablespoons cold water

For the filling
75g dark brown sugar
75g butter, softened
3 eggs, lightly beaten
1 teaspoon cornflour
160ml golden syrup
160ml maple syrup
4 tablespoons bourbon
1 teaspoon vanilla extract
175g chopped pecans or walnuts

For the bourbon cream
240ml double cream
2 tablespoons bourbon
1 tablespoon dark brown sugar

1 Sift the flour and salt into a mixing bowl. Add the butter and rub it in until the mixture resembles breadcrumbs. Sprinkle over the water and mix to a firm dough. Knead briefly, then wrap in cling film and chill for 30 minutes.

2 Put a baking sheet in the oven and preheat to 200°C/400°F/Gas mark 6. Roll out the pastry on a floured surface and use to line a 23cm tart tin. Prick the base all over and chill for 10 minutes.

3 Line the pastry case with non-stick baking paper and fill with baking beans. Bake for 15 minutes. Remove the paper and beans, brush the base with 1 teaspoon beaten egg from the filling and bake for 5 minutes. Reduce the oven temperature to 180°C/350°F/Gas mark 4.

4 Beat the sugar and butter until creamy. Gradually beat in the eggs and cornflour. Stir in the syrups, Bourbon, vanilla extract and nuts. Pour into the pastry case and bake for 35–40 minutes, or until the filling is just set.

5 For the cream, whip the cream, Bourbon and sugar together in a bowl until soft peaks form. Serve the pie warm with the cream.

Fig & Ricotta Tart

Serves 6–8

175g plain flour
80g ground rice
200g unsalted butter
100g caster sugar

For the filling
500g ricotta cheese
75g icing sugar
2 teaspoons vanilla extract
6 ripe figs, quartered
2 tablespoons clear honey

1 Mix the flour and ground rice together. Cream the butter and sugar together in another bowl until light and fluffy. Mix in the flour and ground rice and bring together to form a ball.

2 Press the pastry into the base of a 23cm loose-bottomed tart tin. Prick with a fork and chill for 20 minutes. Meanwhile, preheat the oven to 180°C/350°F/Gas mark 4.

3 Bake for 20-25 minutes. Leave to cool completely, then remove from the tart tin.

4 For the filling, beat the ricotta cheese, icing sugar and vanilla extract together in a bowl. Spread the mixture over the shortbread base and arrange the figs over the ricotta. Drizzle with honey just before serving.

Tarte Fine aux Pommes

Serves 4-6

Butter, for greasing
350g ready-made puff pastry,
   thawed if frozen
Plain flour, for dusting

For the filling
2 eating apples
1½ tablespoons icing sugar
2 tablespoons apricot jam
Cream, to serve

Tip
Puff pastry has a high
fat content, which makes
it fragile compared
with other pastries so
try not to handle it
too much.

1. Preheat the oven to 190°C/375°F/Gas mark 5 and lightly grease a baking sheet. Roll the pastry out thinly on a lightly floured surface and cut out a 23cm round. Transfer to the prepared baking sheet.

2. Halve and core the apples and thinly slice lengthways. Lay on the pastry in concentric circles, overlapping slightly and leaving a 1cm margin around the edge. Dust with the icing sugar.

3. Transfer the baking sheet to the oven and bake for 20-25 minutes, or until the pastry is risen and golden and the apples are tender and golden at the edges.

4. Gently heat the apricot jam in a small saucepan, then press through a sieve to remove any large pieces. While the jam and tart are both hot, brush the jam generously over the apple slices. Leave to cool slightly and serve warm with cream.

Honey & Mixed Nut Tart

Serves 8

190g plain flour, plus extra for dusting
Pinch of salt
100g cold butter, diced
2–3 tablespoons cold water
Double cream, to serve

For the filling
100g butter
240ml clear honey
275g mixed nuts, such as pecan nuts,
   walnuts, hazelnuts and almonds

1 Sift the flour and salt into a mixing bowl. Add the butter and rub it in until the mixture resembles fine breadcrumbs. Add 2 tablespoons water and mix to a firm dough, adding more water, if needed. Knead briefly, then wrap in cling film and chill for 20 minutes.

2 Roll out the pastry on a floured surface to a rough round at least 5cm larger than a loose-bottomed 23cm fluted tart tin. Prick the base all over with a fork. Chill for 20 minutes.

3 Put a baking sheet in the oven and preheat to 200°C/400°F/Gas mark 6. Line the pastry case with non-stick baking paper and fill with baking beans. Bake blind for 12 minutes, then remove the paper and beans and bake for 10 minutes, or until pale golden. Cool on a wire rack. Reduce the oven temperature to 190°C/375°F/Gas mark 5.

4 Heat the butter and honey gently until melted, then increase the heat and let bubble for 1-2 minutes, or until starting to darken. Stir in the nuts and return to simmering point. Cool slightly.

5 Pour the filling into the pastry case and bake for 5-7 minutes, or until the nuts are golden and the pastry is browned. Serve warm with cream.

Orange Chiffon Pie

Serves 6–8

18–20 digestive biscuits, finely crushed
50g butter, melted
2 tablespoons caster sugar (optional)
Whipped cream, to serve

For the filling
60ml cold water
1 packet or 1 tablespoon gelatine
4 eggs, separated
275g caster sugar
Grated zest of 1 orange
120ml freshly squeezed orange juice
$\frac{1}{4}$ teaspoon cream of tartar

To decorate
Julienne strips of orange zest
 simmered in water until tender

1 Combine the crushed biscuits, melted butter and sugar, if using, in a large bowl. Pour into a 23cm pie tin and, using a 20cm pie tin, press the crumbs firmly against the base and sides of the larger tin. Alternatively, use the back of a tablespoon to press the crumbs against the base and sides of the pan. Chill until firm.

2 For the filling, pour the water into a coffee cup or a small bowl, sprinkle over the gelatine and leave to stand for 10 minutes. Set the cup in a saucepan of simmering water and heat gently for 5 minutes, stirring, until the gelatine has dissolved.

3 Using an electric beater, beat the egg yolks in a large heatproof bowl for 1-2 minutes until light and fluffy. Gradually beat in half the sugar, the grated orange zest and juice. Set the bowl over a saucepan of simmering water (the base of the bowl should just touch the water) and cook, stirring, for about 8-10 minutes, until the mixture thickens and coats the back of a wooden spoon. Remove the bowl from the water, stir in the gelatine mixture and cool the custard, stirring occasionally.

4 Using clean beaters, whisk the egg whites and cream of tartar in a large clean bowl until fluffy. Increase the speed and whisk until soft peaks form. Gradually whisk in the remaining sugar until the whites are stiff and glossy.

5 Beat a spoonful of the whites into the custard, then pour the mixture over the whites and fold together until the mixtures are just blended. Pour into the tin, mounding the mixture in the middle and chill for 4-6 hours until set. Decorate with orange zest and serve with whipped cream.

Banana Cream Pie

Serves 8

225g vanilla wafer crumbs
65g butter, melted

For the filling
40g cornflour
90g caster sugar
450ml milk
240ml single cream
30g butter
3 egg yolks
½ teaspoon vanilla extract
3 medium bananas
2 tablespoons orange juice

For the topping
160ml double cream
1 tablespoon icing sugar, sifted
½ teaspoon vanilla extract

1 Mix the wafer crumbs and melted butter together, and press the mixture evenly over the base and up the sides of a 20–23cm pie dish. Chill while making the filling.

2 For the filling, blend the cornflour, sugar and a little of the milk into a paste in a saucepan, then stir in the remaining milk and cream. Add the butter and cook over a low heat, stirring continuously, until the mixture boils and thickens. Simmer for a further 1 minute.

3 Remove the pan from the heat and leave to cool for 1 minute. Mix the egg yolks in a bowl, then stir in a large spoonful of the custard mixture. Stir the egg mixture into the custard mixture, then stir in the vanilla extract. Return to a very low heat and cook for about 5 minutes until the mixture has thickened slightly. Do not let the custard boil or it may curdle.

4 Slice 2 bananas and toss in the orange juice. Remove them from the juice, reserving the juice, and use to cover the base of the pastry case. Pour the custard over the bananas. Leave to cool, then chill for 2 hours.

5 For the topping, whip the cream, icing sugar and vanilla extract until soft peaks form. Spoon and spread the cream in the centre of the pie, leaving a border of custard showing.

6 Slice the remaining banana and toss in the orange juice. Arrange in an overlapping circle on top of the cream and serve at once.

Marlborough Pie

Serves 8

175g plain flour, plus extra for dusting
½ teaspoon ground cinnamon
2 tablespoons caster sugar
115g butter or half butter/half white
    vegetable fat, diced
1 egg yolk
2–3 teaspoons cold water

For the filling

350g cooking or tart apples, peeled,
    cored and roughly chopped
2 tablespoons butter
1 tablespoon lemon juice and finely
    grated zest of ½ a small lemon
50g light brown sugar
120ml double cream
2 egg yolks
50g raisins
75g chopped toasted walnuts or
    pecans nuts

For the meringue topping

3 egg whites
200g icing sugar, sifted
½ teaspoon vanilla extract

1 Sift the flour and cinnamon into a bowl. Stir in the sugar. Add the butter and rub it in until the mixture resembles breadcrumbs. Mix the egg yolk with 2 teaspoons water and sprinkle over the dry ingredients. Mix to a firm dough, adding extra water if needed. Knead, wrap and chill for 30 minutes.

2 Put a baking sheet in the oven and preheat to 200°C/400°F/Gas mark 6. Roll out the pastry and use to line a 23cm tart tin. Prick the base and chill for 10 minutes. Line the pastry case with non-stick baking paper and fill with baking beans. Bake blind for 15 minutes. Remove the paper and beans and bake for 5 minutes. Leave to cool. Reduce the oven temperature to 160°C/325°F/Gas mark 3.

3 Heat the apples, butter and lemon juice gently until tender and pulpy. Press through a sieve into a jug. Add the lemon zest and sugar and stir until dissolved. Mix in the cream, then the egg yolks. For the topping, beat the egg whites until peaks form, then set over a pan of simmering water. Add the sugar and vanilla. Beat until thick. Remove from the heat and beat for 2 minutes.

4 Sprinkle the raisins and nuts over the base of the case, then pour in the filling. Spread the meringue on top. Bake for 30 minutes, or until the meringue is dark golden and crisp.

Freeform Spiced Plum Pie

Serves 6–8

75g pecan nuts, very
  finely chopped
200g plain flour, plus extra for dusting
150g unsalted butter, diced
120ml soured cream
Whipped cream, to serve

For the filling
900g ripe plums, stoned and quartered
115g light brown sugar
1 teaspoon ground cinnamon
½ teaspoon ground ginger
Pinch of freshly grated nutmeg

Tip

Always flour the work
surface and rolling pin lightly
before rolling out the pastry to
prevent it sticking. You can always
sprinkle extra flour on to the
rolling pin or work surface
if it is starting to stick.

1 Put the pecan nuts, flour and butter in a food processor and process briefly until the mixture forms very coarse breadcrumbs. Add the soured cream and process for a further 4–5 seconds. Alternatively, rub the butter into the flour using your hands or a pastry cutter and mix in the cream.

2 Turn the pastry out on to a lightly floured board and bring the mixture together with your hands. Wrap in cling film and leave to chill for 20 minutes.

3 For the filling, put the plums in a bowl and mix with the brown sugar and spices.

4 Roll out the pastry on a lightly floured surface into a round 35cm in diameter, and put on a non-stick baking sheet. Pile the plums into the centre of the pastry, leaving a 7.5cm margin.

5 Bring up the sides of the pastry to half-cover the plums, then leave the pie to chill for 20 minutes. Preheat the oven to 200°C/400°F/Gas mark 6, then bake for 40–45 minutes. Serve with whipped cream.

Caramel Cream Pie

Serves 8

175g plain flour, plus extra for dusting
Pinch of salt
90g chilled butter, diced
2–3 tablespoons water

For the filling
2 eggs, lightly beaten
115g caster sugar
80ml hot water
400ml milk
50g butter
40g plain flour
150g light brown sugar
3 tablespoons double cream

For the topping
240ml double cream
1 tablespoon light brown sugar
Pinch of cream of tartar

1 Sift the flour and salt into a mixing bowl. Add the butter and rub it in until the mixture resembles fine breadcrumbs. Sprinkle over the water and mix to a firm dough, adding a little extra water if necessary. Knead briefly, then wrap in cling film and chill for 30 minutes.

2 Put a baking sheet in the oven and preheat to 200°C/400°F/Gas mark 6. Roll out the pastry on a lightly floured surface and use to line a 23cm tart tin. Prick the base and chill for 10 minutes.

3 Line the pastry case with non-stick baking paper and fill with baking beans. Bake blind for 15 minutes. Remove the paper and beans, brush the base with 1 teaspoon beaten egg from the filling, and bake for 5 minutes. Reduce the oven temperature to 160°C/325°F/Gas mark 3.

4 Put the sugar and 2 tablespoons water in a saucepan over a low heat. When the sugar has dissolved, increase the heat and cook, without stirring, until it is dark golden. Remove from the heat and carefully pour in the hot water. Cool slightly, then stir in the milk. Melt the butter in another pan, then remove from the heat and stir in the flour and brown sugar. Stir in the eggs, then the caramel mixture and cream. Cook over a low heat, stirring, until the mixture thickens, but do not boil.

5 Pour the filling into the pastry case and bake for 20 minutes, or until lightly set. Leave on a wire rack until cold. Chill for 2 hours. Pour the cream into a chilled bowl and stir in the sugar and cream of tartar. Whip until soft peaks form, then spread over the filling.

Blacksmith Pie

Serves 6–8

75g butter
175g chocolate-covered digestive
    biscuits, crushed
1 teaspoon cocoa powder

For the filling
3 tablespoons cornflour
200g caster sugar, plus 2 tablespoons
240ml milk
120ml single cream
2 egg yolks
1 egg
75g plain chocolate chips
300ml double cream
1 teaspoon vanilla extract
2 egg whites

1 Line the base of a 20–21cm round loose-bottomed tin with non-stick baking paper. Melt the butter in a saucepan, then stir in the biscuit crumbs and mix together. Press over the base and sides of the tin. Chill while making the filling.

2 Combine the cornflour, the 2 tablespoons sugar, milk and single cream in a saucepan. Stir over a low heat with a whisk until thickened and smooth. Turn off the heat.

3 Beat the egg yolks and egg together. Stir in a spoonful of hot custard, then stir the egg mixture into the rest of the custard in the pan. Slowly bring to the boil, stirring, until slightly thickened.

4 Transfer 240ml of the hot custard to a bowl. Add the chocolate chips and stir until melted. Spoon into the pastry case, spreading over the base and slightly up the sides. Chill.

5 Cover the remaining custard with dampened baking paper and leave to cool. Beat the double cream, vanilla extract and half the sugar until soft peaks form. Beat the egg whites in a clean, grease-free bowl until stiff, then gradually beat in the remaining sugar.

6 Stir the custard until smooth. Fold in the whipped cream and meringue mixture. Pour into the pastry case and chill for at least 1 hour. Dust with the cocoa powder before serving.

Pear Tart with Walnut

& Star Anise

Serves 6

225g plain flour, plus extra for dusting
Pinch of salt
2 egg yolks
115g butter, plus extra for greasing
3 tablespoons caster sugar
Beaten egg, for glazing

For the filling
150g caster sugar
425ml water
6 whole star anise
7 small, firm, just-ripe pears
2 tablespoons lemon juice
1 egg, beaten
6 whole cloves
Large strip pared lemon zest, cut into
    fine shreds
25g walnut halves

1 Sift the flour and salt on to a work surface. Make a well in the centre. Add the egg yolks, butter and sugar and work these together. Gradually work in the flour. Knead, then wrap and chill for 1 hour.

2 Put the sugar, water and 2 star anise in a saucepan. Heat until the sugar dissolves, then bring to the boil and simmer for 1 minute. Halve and peel the pears. Scoop out the core, then brush each half with lemon juice. Add to the syrup, cover and leave to simmer for 20 minutes, or until tender, turning occasionally.

3 Preheat the oven to 190°C/375°F/Gas mark 5 and grease a baking sheet. Roll out the pastry on a lightly floured surface and cut out a 25cm round. Put on a the baking sheet and push the edge of the pastry in slightly to form a thicker pie edge. Prick the base all over. Re-roll the pastry trimmings and cut out star shapes with a small cutter. Arrange around the edge, attaching with beaten egg. Brush with beaten egg, then bake for 12–15 minutes.

4 Arrange the cooked pears cut-side up in the pastry case. Add the remaining star anise, cloves, zest and walnuts to the syrup. Bring to a rapid boil for 5 minutes, until thickened. Strain the syrup, reserve and scatter the star anise, zest and walnuts on top of the pears. Drizzle over a little syrup and serve hot.

Chocolate Chip
& Peanut Butter Pie

Serves 8

175g plain flour, plus extra for dusting
Pinch of salt
90g chilled butter, diced
2 tablespoons cold water

For the filling
3 eggs, lightly beaten
115g smooth peanut butter
115g brown sugar
200g golden syrup
1 teaspoon vanilla extract
100g plain chocolate chips

1 Sift the flour and salt into a mixing bowl. Add the butter and rub it in until the mixture resembles fine breadcrumbs. Sprinkle over the water and mix to a firm dough. Knead briefly, then wrap in cling film and chill for 30 minutes.

2 Roll out the pastry on a lightly floured surface and use to line a shallow 23cm pie dish. Prick the base all over with a fork, then crimp the edge or decorate with the fork. Chill for 10 minutes.

3 Put a baking sheet in the oven and preheat to 200°C/400°F/Gas mark 6. Line the pastry case with non-stick baking paper and fill with baking beans. Bake for 15 minutes. Remove the paper and beans, brush the base with 1 teaspoon beaten egg from the filling, and bake for a further 5 minutes. Reduce the oven temperature to 180°C/350°F/Gas mark 4.

4 For the filling, combine the peanut butter, sugar, syrup, eggs and vanilla extract in a bowl. Stir in the chocolate chips. Pour the filling into the pastry case and bake for 30 minutes. The centre will still be slightly wobbly, but will firm up as it cools.

5 Remove from the oven and leave to stand for 15 minutes on a wire rack, then remove the pie from the tin and cool before serving.

Frangipani Cream Pie

Serves 8

200g puff pastry, thawed if frozen
Plain flour, for dusting
115g ground almonds
115g caster sugar
50g butter, softened
3 eggs, lightly beaten
1 tablespoon plain flour
3 tablespoons apricot jam

For the topping
160ml double cream
2 tablespoons icing sugar, sifted
2 drops almond extract

1 Roll out the pastry on a lightly floured surface, and use to line a 23cm pie dish. Prick the base all over with a fork and knock up the edge of the pastry with the back of a knife. Chill in the refrigerator while making the filling.

2 Put a baking sheet in the oven and preheat to 200°C/400°F/Gas mark 6. Put the almonds, sugar and butter in a bowl and beat together. Gradually beat in the eggs a little at a time. Sift over the flour and stir in, together with 1 tablespoon of the cream from the topping.

3 Spread the jam over the base of the pastry case, then spoon the filling over the jam and spread it out evenly. Bake for 30 minutes, or until the filling is set and the pastry browned and crisp.

4 Chill the pie in the refrigerator for 1 hour. For the topping, pour the cream into a chilled bowl and stir in 1 tablespoon of the icing sugar and the almond extract. Whip until soft peaks form, then spoon into a piping bag and pipe swirls of cream around the edge of the pie. Dust with the remaining icing sugar before serving.

Figgy Meringue Tarts

Makes 4

2 egg whites
120g caster sugar
4 individual deep custard tarts
4 ripe figs

1 Preheat the oven to 220°C/425°F/Gas mark 7.

2 Whisk the egg whites in a clean, grease-free bowl until stiff. Gradually whisk in the sugar a little at a time, whisking well between each addition until the mixture is thick and glossy.

3 Arrange the custard tarts on a baking sheet and bake for 6–8 minutes until warmed through. Remove from the oven and top each with a fig.

4 Spoon the meringue mixture evenly over each fig to cover them completely. Using the tip of a knife to gently pull the meringue into peaks. Bake for 4–5 minutes until lightly golden and just warm.

Tip

When buying figs, always look for ones that are soft and have a sweet aroma. Avoid any that look too soft.

Apple & Cinnamon Pie

Serves 6–8

225g plain flour, plus extra for dusting
Pinch of salt
120g cold unsalted butter, diced
55g caster sugar
2–3 tablespoons cold water
Milk, for brushing

For the filling
55–75g caster sugar, plus extra for
    sprinkling
1 teaspoon ground cinnamon
1kg dessert apples, peeled, cored and
    thinly sliced

1 Sift the flour and salt into a mixing bowl. Add the butter and rub it in until the mixture resembles breadcrumbs. Add the sugar, then sprinkle over the water and mix to a firm dough. Knead, wrap in cling film and chill for 30 minutes.

2 Preheat the oven to 200°C/400°F/Gas mark 6. Divide the pastry into 2 pieces. Roll out one piece on a lightly floured surface into a 25cm diameter round and use to line a 23cm pie tin.

3 Mix the sugar and cinnamon together in a bowl and sprinkle over the sliced apples. Arrange the apple slices in the tin – don't worry if the apples are above the top of the tin.

4 Roll out the remaining pastry into a 25cm diameter round. Brush the edge of the pastry in the tin with a little milk. Carefully lay the pastry over the apples and press down the edges to seal. Trim off any excess pastry and decorate the edge with a fork, if liked. Make 2 slashes in the top of the pie, or prick with a fork a couple of times.

5 Brush the top of the pastry with a little milk, then sprinkle with sugar. Bake in the centre of the oven for 25-30 minutes until the pastry is golden and the apples are tender. Serve warm or cold.

Black Bottom Cream Pie

Serves 8

115g plain flour
3 tablespoons cocoa powder
2 tablespoons icing sugar
75g chilled butter, diced
1 egg yolk
1 tablespoon cold water
Grated chocolate, to decorate

For the filling

4 egg yolks
50g caster sugar
4 teaspoons cornflour
400ml milk
55g plain chocolate
1 tablespoon dark rum

For the topping

1½ teaspoon powdered gelatine
2 tablespoons cold water
120ml double cream
2 tablespoons dark rum
3 egg whites
40g icing sugar, sifted
½ teaspoon cream of tartar

1 Sift the flour, cocoa and icing sugar into a bowl. Add the butter and rub it in until the mixture resembles breadcrumbs. Mix the egg yolk and water, add to the dry ingredients and mix to a firm dough. Knead, wrap and chill for 30 minutes.

2 Put a baking sheet in the oven and preheat to 200°C/400°F/Gas mark 6. Grease a 23cm pie tin. Roll out the pastry and use to line the tin. Prick the base, line with foil and fill with baking beans. Bake for 15 minutes. Remove the foil and beans and bake for a further 10 minutes. Leave to cool.

3 Beat the egg yolks, caster sugar and cornflour together. Bring the milk to the boil, then pour over the egg mixture, beating. Return to a low heat and stir until thick. Remove from the heat and stir in the chocolate until melted, then the rum. Spoon into the case and cool. Sprinkle the gelatine over the water and soak for 5 minutes. Set the bowl over a pan of simmering water and stir until dissolved. Cool slightly. Whip the cream until soft peaks form, then beat in the gelatine and rum. Chill for 30 minutes.

4 Beat the egg whites until stiff, then beat in the icing sugar, a tablespoon at a time, with the cream of tartar. Fold into the cream mixture, then spoon on top of the pie. Chill until set, then decorate with grated chocolate.

Raspberry & Coconut Pie

Serves 8

250g plain flour, plus extra for dusting
Pinch of salt
75g cold unsalted butter, diced
55g white vegetable fat
2–3 tablespoons cold water

For the filling
175g unsalted butter
200g caster sugar
3 eggs, beaten
275g desiccated coconut
4 tablespoons raspberry jam

Tip

When lining the tart tin with the pastry, ease the pastry carefully into the tin. Do not pull or stretch the pastry, otherwise it may tear. It if does, just moisten the edges with a little water and gently press together.

1 Sift the flour and salt into a mixing bowl. Add the butter and fat and rub it in until the mixture resembles fine breadcrumbs. Add 2 tablespoons water and mix to a firm dough, adding a little more water, if necessary. Knead briefly, then wrap in cling film and chill for 20 minutes.

2 Roll out the pastry on a lightly floured surface and use to line a rectangular 30 x 20cm loose-bottomed tart tin. Prick the base with a fork and chill for 10 minutes.

3 Put a baking sheet in the oven and preheat to 190°C/375°F/Gas mark 5.

4 For the filling, beat the butter and sugar together in a bowl until light and fluffy. Slowly beat in the eggs, then fold in the desiccated coconut.

5 Spread the jam over the pastry base and spoon the coconut mixture on top, levelling out the surface. Bake for 35–40 minutes. Leave to cool a little, then cut into slices.

Lemon Chiffon Pie

Serves 6–8

175g plain flour, plus extra for dusting
Pinch of salt
85g butter, diced
50g caster sugar
2 teaspoons grated lemon zest
2 tablespoons cold water
1 egg yolk

For the filling
200g caster sugar
3 eggs
Grated zest and juice of 3 large lemons
75g butter
2 egg whites

1 Sift the flour and salt into a mixing bowl. Add the butter and rub it in until the mixture resembles breadcrumbs. Stir in the sugar and lemon zest. Mix the water and egg yolk together and add to the bowl. Mix to a firm dough. Knead, wrap and chill for 30 minutes.

2 Preheat the oven to 200°C/400°F/Gas mark 6. Roll out the pastry on a lightly floured surface and use to line a 23cm tart tin. Prick the base all over, then chill for 15 minutes. Line the pastry case with non-stick baking paper and fill with baking beans. Bake blind for 10 minutes. Remove the paper and beans and bake for 5 minutes. Reduce the oven temperature to 150°C/300°F/Gas mark 2.

3 Whisk half the sugar, the eggs, the lemon zest and juice and butter together in a heatproof bowl. Put the bowl over a saucepan of simmering water and whisk for 15 minutes until thick. Put the base of the bowl into cold water. Whisk until cool. Beat the egg whites in a clean bowl until stiff, then gradually beat in the remaining sugar until thick and shiny. Fold a large spoonful of the mixture into the lemon mixture, then fold in the remaining egg whites. Pour into the pastry case.

4 Bake in the centre of the oven for 25–30 minutes until just set. Cool before serving.

Cherry Pie

Serves 6–8

375g plain flour, plus extra for dusting
½ teaspoon salt
125g unsalted butter, diced
120g white vegetable fat
2–3 tablespoons cold water
Milk, for brushing

For the filling
800g stoned fresh or canned cherries
50g caster sugar, plus extra for
   sprinkling
2 teaspoons cornflour
½ teaspoon ground cinnamon
Pinch of freshly grated nutmeg

1 Sift the flour and salt into a mixing bowl. Add the butter and fat and rub it in until the mixture resembles fine breadcrumbs. Add 2 tablespoons water and mix to a firm dough, adding more water, if necessary. Knead briefly, then wrap in cling film and chill for 20 minutes.

2 Preheat the oven to 200°C/400°F/Gas mark 6. For the filling, mix the cherries, sugar, cornflour and spices together in a bowl.

3 Divide the pastry into 2 pieces, one a little larger than the other. Roll out the larger piece of pastry on a lightly floured surface and use to line a 20 x 4cm diameter deep tin. Spoon the filling into the tin. Brush the edges of the pastry with milk.

4 Roll out the remaining pastry and use to make a lid, pressing the edges together to seal. Trim the excess pastry and crimp or score the edges. Score the surface of the pie to decorate. Chill for 20 minutes, then brush the top with extra milk and sprinkle with sugar.

5 Bake for 45 minutes, or until golden. Leave to stand for 5 minutes before serving.

FRUITY FAVOURITES

- Apricot & Banana Crumble
- Apple & Raisin Crumble
- Fruity Meringue Crush
- Strawberry Cheesecake
- Peach, Pecan, Caramel Waffles
- Summer Berry Crêpes
- Blueberry & White Chocolate Meringue Roll
- Upside-down Pear Tart with Cardamom
- Rhubarb, Orange & Ginger Fool
- Berry Shortcake
- Candied Fruit Bombe
- Fried Bananas with Rum & Brown Sugar
- Cherry Syllabub
- Prunes Steeped in Tea with Vanilla
- Sweet & Nutty Caramel Strawberries
- Pineapple Upside-down Cake
- Summer Berry Galette
- Muscat-poached Grapes with Thick Creamy Yogurt
- Spiced Baked Apples
- Strawberries in Pimm's Syrup with Shortbread
- Orange Terrine with Citrus Cream
- Fresh Figs Baked
- Raspberry Surprise
- Tropical Fruit Salad
- Blackcurrant Pudding
- Tarte Tatin
- Berry Polenta Cake
- Seared Fruit in Frothy Orange Sauce
- Gooseberry Pie
- Pavlova with Tropical Fruits

CHAPTER FIVE

FRUITY
FAVOURITES

Apricot & Banana Crumble

Serves 4-6

250g dried apricots
250ml fresh orange juice
4 bananas
¼ teaspoon ground cinnamon
¼ teaspoon ground dried ginger
Single cream or custard, to serve

For the topping
200g plain flour
115g light brown sugar
120g unsalted butter

Tip

For a crunchier topping, add 50g each of rolled oats and chopped hazelnuts to the crumble mix in step 3.

1 Soak the apricots in the orange juice for 2 hours until they have plumped up.

2 Preheat the oven to 200°C/400°F/Gas mark 6. Carefully slice the bananas into 1cm rounds and mix with the apricots and spices. Put in an ovenproof dish.

3 For the topping, mix the flour and brown sugar together in a bowl. Add the butter and rub it in until it forms coarse breadcrumbs. Sprinkle the mixture over the fruit.

4 Cook in the oven for 35-40 minutes until golden. Serve warm with cream or custard.

Apple & Raisin Crumble

Serves 4

175g plain flour
Pinch of salt
115g unsalted butter, diced
50g rolled oats
75g soft light brown sugar
1kg dessert apples
50g raisins
Single cream, to serve

1 Preheat the oven to 200°C/400°F/Gas mark 6.
Put the flour and salt in a mixing bowl. Add the
butter and rub it in until the mixture resembles
coarse breadcrumbs – a few large lumps of butter
are fine.

2 Stir in the oats and sugar. Peel the apples,
quarter lengthways and core them. Slice the
apples very thinly and put them into an ovenproof
dish. Scatter over the raisins. Spoon over the flour
mixture to cover the fruit evenly. Transfer to the
oven and cook for 25–30 minutes. Serve warm or
cold with single cream.

Tip
Crumbles are a good all-round
family sweet dish, which can be varied
not just by using fruits in season, but also
by ringing the changes with the crumble
topping. Whatever problems you may
have with your pastry-making technique,
you're absolutely safe with a crumble
because there is no resting or
roll-out involved.

Fruity Meringue Crush

Serves 2

2 ready-made meringue nests
150g Greek yoghurt
5 strawberries, hulled and halved,
 plus extra to decorate

1 Roughly crush the meringue nests and reserve on a plate. Put the yoghurt in a bowl and gently fold in the crushed meringue nests and strawberries.

2 Scatter a few extra strawberries on top to decorate and serve immediately with 2 spoons.

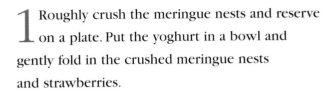

Tip
You can make
this fabulous dessert
using other fruits too. Try it
with raspberries or sliced
peaches in place of the
strawberries, if you
prefer.

Strawberry Cheesecake

Serves 10–12

For the base
Sunflower oil, for oiling
225g digestive biscuits, finely crushed
50g butter, melted
50g candied peel, very finely chopped (optional)

For the filling
600g full-fat cream cheese
175g caster sugar
1 teaspoon vanilla extract
300ml whipping cream, whipped to soft peaks

For the topping
500g strawberries, hulled
2–3 tablespoons icing sugar, to taste
Juice of ½ lemon

1 For the base, lightly oil a 20cm springform cake tin. Mix the biscuit crumbs with the melted butter and candied peel, if using. Spread in an even layer over the base of the tin and press down well. Chill while you make the filling.

2 For the filling, beat the cheese, sugar and vanilla extract together until smooth. Carefully fold in the whipped cream, taking care not to overbeat or the mixture will separate. Spread this mixture on top of the biscuit base and level the surface. Chill for at least 4 hours, or preferably overnight.

3 For the topping, put 150g of the strawberries, icing sugar and lemon juice in a food processor and process to a purée. Press through a sieve to remove the seeds. Halve the remaining strawberries and put into a bowl with the puréed strawberries. Mix together. Taste and add more strawberries. Mix together, then taste and add more icing sugar if necessary.

4 To serve, loosen the tin and remove the outer ring and put on to a large serving plate. Spoon the strawberry purée over the top, allowing a little to run down the sides. Top with the remaining strawberries and cut into small wedges (if it's very rich) and serve.

Peach, Pecan, Caramel

Waffles

Makes 8–10 waffles

225g plain flour
2 teaspoons baking powder
1 teaspoon bicarbonate of soda
2 eggs
50g melted butter
175ml milk
284ml carton buttermilk
1 teaspoon vanilla extract

To serve
2 peaches
75g pecan nuts, chopped
1 tablespoon light brown sugar
5 tablespoons maple syrup
3 tablespoons dark rum

1 For the waffles, sift the dry ingredients into a large bowl. Whisk in the eggs, butter and milk, gradually incorporating the flour until smooth.

2 Add the buttermilk and vanilla extract to the mixture. Cover and leave to stand for 30 minutes. Heat a hand-held or electric waffle iron and pour a ladleful over two-thirds of the iron. Close it and wipe off any excess batter.

3 Cook for 3–4 minutes, following the manufacturer's instructions.

4 When the batter stops steaming, open the iron and lift out the waffle with a fork. Keep hot in the oven.

5 Preheat the grill. Slice the peaches into wedges and spread over a baking tray. Scatter the pecans over the top, then sprinkle over the brown sugar. Drizzle with the maple syrup and dark rum and cook under the hot grill until the sugar is bubbling and the pecans are golden.

6 Spoon the peaches and pecans on top of the waffles and drizzle over some of the juices.

Summer Berry Crêpes

Serves 4

100g plain flour
Pinch of salt
1 large egg
300ml milk
A few drops of vanilla extract
4 tablespoons water
15g butter
1 tablespoon sunflower oil
Whipped cream to serve

For the fruit
15g butter
50g caster sugar
1 teaspoon grated orange zest
5 tablespoons fresh orange juice
350g mixed summer fruits, such as
  strawberries, raspberries,
  blueberries
2 tablespoons white rum

To decorate
Fresh fruit or mint leaves
Strips of orange zest

1 Sift the flour and salt into a mixing bowl and make a well in the centre. Break in the egg and gradually add half the milk, whisking briskly to draw the flour into the egg.

2 Whisk in the remaining milk, vanilla extract and the water to make a smooth batter which has the consistency of single cream.

3 Heat a small, non-stick frying pan and add the butter and oil. When the butter has melted, pour into a small bowl and return the pan to the heat. Add a small ladleful of the batter mixture and swirl around the base of the pan until evenly coated. Cook until golden, then flip over and cook on the other side, 1–2 minutes in total. Slide the crêpe on to a plate. Repeat with the remaining batter, adding a little of the butter and oil mixture between crêpes.

4 For the fruit, melt the butter in a saucepan, stir in the sugar and cook gently for 1–2 minutes until golden brown. Add the orange zest and juice and swirl the pan until the sugar has dissolved. Add the fruit and rum and cook until the fruit juices begin to run. Fold 2 crêpes on to each serving plate and top with a spoonful of the fruit. Decorate with fresh fruit or mint and strips of orange zest and serve with cream, if liked.

Blueberry & White

Chocolate Meringue Roll

Serves 6

275g caster sugar
½ vanilla pod
5 egg whites
Icing sugar for dusting

For the filling
150g white chocolate
100ml natural yoghurt
250g mascarpone cheese
100g blueberries

1 Preheat the oven to 220°C/425°F/Gas mark 7. Grease and line a 23 x 33cm Swiss roll tin with greaseproof paper.

2 Combine the caster sugar and the seeds from inside the vanilla pod. Whisk the egg whites in a clean, grease-free bowl until stiff. Gradually whisk in the vanilla sugar a spoonful at a time until it forms a stiff, glossy meringue.

3 Spread the meringue mixture into the prepared tin and bake for 8 minutes. Reduce the oven temperature to 160°C/325°F/Gas mark 3 and continue cooking for 10 minutes, or until firm to the touch.

4 Remove the meringue from the oven and turn out on to a sheet of baking parchment dusted with icing sugar. Peel off the lining paper from the base and leave to cool for 10 minutes.

5 Meanwhile, for the filling, melt the chocolate in a bowl set over a saucepan of simmering water. Stir in the yoghurt, then beat into the mascarpone. Spread the cream over the meringue and top with the blueberries. Roll up from one of the long sides using the paper underneath to help. Leave wrapped in the paper for at least 1 hour before serving, dusted with icing sugar.

Upside-down Pear Tart
with Cardamom

Serves 4–6

125g caster sugar
3–4 tablespoons cold water
About 10 green cardamom pods
4–6 ripe but firm pears, depending on
   size, cored and quartered lengthways
50g unsalted butter, diced
450g ready-made puff pastry
Plain flour, for dusting
Crème fraîche or soured cream to
   serve

1 Put the sugar and water into a 25cm ovenproof frying pan. Stir over a low heat until the sugar has dissolved completely. Increase the heat and bring the mixture to a rapid simmer.

2 Remove the seeds from the cardamoms and finely crush. As soon as the sugar begins to colour, sprinkle over the cardamom seeds. Do not stir. Carefully add the pear quarters in concentric circles. The sugar will slow down, but you must watch it now as you want it to colour evenly. Tilt and turn the pan often until the sugar bubbling up

between the pears is deep brown and smells nutty. Immediately remove from the heat and add butter wherever there are spaces between the fruit. Leave to cool for about 20 minutes.

3 Preheat the oven to 200°C/400°F/Gas mark 6. Roll out the prepared puff pastry thinly on a lightly floured surface, then cut a round about 2.5cm larger than the diameter of the frying pan. Carefully put the pastry over the pears, tucking it down the sides of the pan to enclose the fruit.

4 Transfer the frying pan to the oven and bake for 25 minutes until the pastry is risen and golden brown.

5 Remove from the oven and leave to stand for about 10 minutes before turning out. Serve warm, cut into wedges, with crème fraîche or soured cream.

Rhubarb, Orange
& Ginger Fool

Serves 4–6

400g young rhubarb
1 orange
50g clear honey
2 tablespoons brown sugar
2 pieces stem ginger in syrup
225g ready-made fresh custard
125ml double cream

1 Roughly chop the rhubarb and put in a saucepan. Grate the zest from the orange and add to the rhubarb. Peel off the skin and finely chop the flesh.

2 Add the honey and sugar to the rhubarb. Cover and cook for 10–15 minutes until the rhubarb is tender. Pour into a large bowl and leave to cool. Finely chop the stem ginger and stir in, along with the orange flesh.

3 Whip the custard and cream together and pour over the fruit. Chill until ready to serve.

Tip
You can also serve this dessert in individual glasses, decorated with toasted nuts and served with amaretti biscuits.

Berry Shortcake

Makes 8 shortcakes

675g strawberries, hulled and
sliced, or a mixture of strawberries,
raspberries, blueberries and
blackberries
2–3 tablespoons caster sugar
1–2 tablespoons raspberry juice or
1 tablespoon orange juice
250ml double cream, whipped until
soft peaks formed and chilled

For the shortcake
225g plain flour, plus extra for dusting
2½ teaspoons baking powder
½ teaspoon salt
2 tablespoons granulated sugar, plus
extra for sprinkling
90g butter, diced
250ml double cream

To decorate
Sliced strawberries
Icing sugar
Fresh mint leaves

1 Preheat the oven to 220°C/425°F/Gas mark 7. Put the berries in a large bowl and toss in the sugar and fruit juice. Leave to stand until the juices begin to run, stirring occasionally.

2 For the shortcake, mix the flour, baking powder, salt and sugar together in a large bowl. Add the butter and rub it in until the mixture resembles coarse breadcrumbs. Whip the cream and, using a fork, lightly stir in all but 1 tablespoon of it, little by little, until a soft dough is formed.

3 Turn out on to a lightly floured work surface and knead the dough 6-8 times. Pat or roll it into a rectangle about 1cm thick. Using a round cutter, stamp out 8 rounds. Arrange 7.5cm apart on a baking sheet. Brush the tops with the remaining cream and sprinkle with sugar.

4 Bake for 10 minutes until set and the tops are pale golden. Leave to cool on a wire rack.

5 Using a fork or serrated knife, split each shortcake horizontally. Put the bottoms on dessert plates and spoon the berry mixture equally over each. Spoon the chilled whipped cream over the berries. Top with the other half of shortcake and decorate each with a sliced strawberry, icing sugar and a mint leaf.

Candied Fruit Bombe

Serves 6

4 tablespoons dark rum or brandy

175g mixed dried fruit, such as
apricots, raisins, figs, cherries and
cranberries, chopped

250ml milk

1 vanilla pod

2 egg yolks

4 tablespoons caster sugar

250ml double cream

55g good-quality plain chocolate,
grated

Fresh mint sprigs, to decorate

Fresh figs, to serve

1 Pour the rum or brandy over the fruit and soak overnight. The next day, heat the milk and vanilla pod to simmering point in a saucepan over a low heat. Take off the heat and remove the vanilla pod. Whisk the egg yolks and sugar with a hand-held electric mixer until pale and slightly thickened, then whisk in the hot milk.

2 Return to a clean heavy-based, non-stick saucepan. Cook over a low heat, stirring continuously with a wooden spoon until the mixture thickens to the consistency of double cream and coats the back of a spoon. Cover with cling film and leave to cool.

3 Lightly whip the cream until soft peaks form, then fold it into the cold custard. Freeze in a shallow freezerproof container for about 2–3 hours, or until half frozen, then whisk to break down any ice crystals and return to the freezer. Repeat this process at least twice more until the ice cream holds its shape. Alternatively, churn in an ice cream maker. Mix in the rum-soaked fruits and the chocolate.

4 Line a 900g pudding basin or 6 individual pudding basins with cling film. Spoon the mixture into the pudding basin and freeze until firm. Remove from the freezer 30 minutes before serving. Turn out and remove the cling film. Decorate with mint sprigs and serve with fresh figs.

Fried Bananas with
Rum & Brown Sugar

Serves 2

50g butter
2 bananas, peeled and
   halved lengthways
2 tablespoons dark rum
2 tablespoons brown sugar
Whipped cream or ice cream,
   to serve

1 Melt the butter in a large frying pan and add the bananas. Fry for 2 minutes on each side, until golden, then add the rum and let bubble.

2 Sprinkle the brown sugar over the top, then reduce the heat, stirring the sauce around the bananas until the sugar has dissolved completely.

3 Increase the heat, and allow the sauce to bubble again for a minute or so, until the sauce is syrupy. Serve with whipped cream or ice cream.

Cherry Syllabub

Serves 4

100ml sweet white wine
50ml white or coconut rum
2 tablespoons fresh lemon juice
90g caster sugar
425ml double cream
300g fresh stoned cherries
Crisp almond biscuits, to serve

Tip
The joy of this dessert is that any flavoured liqueur or spirit of your choice can be added to the basic mixture. Also the fruit can be varied depending on the season and your preference.

1 Combine the white wine, rum, lemon juice and sugar in a large bowl and mix well until the sugar has dissolved.

2 Stir in the cream and whip until soft peaks form. Spoon the cherries into the bases of 4 glasses and top with the cream syllabub.

3 Serve immediately with crisp almond biscuits to dip into the cream. If left to stand for too long the mixture will separate out again.

Prunes Steeped in Tea

with Vanilla

Serves 6

36 large prunes
475ml water
2 heaped teaspoons dark tea leaves,
    such as Ceylon or Assam
120g caster sugar
1 vanilla pod, split in half
    or 1 teaspoon vanilla extract
Vanilla ice cream, to serve (optional)

For the caramelized almonds
100g flaked almonds
50g granulated sugar

Tip
The steeped prunes can be stored in the refrigerator for several days.

1 Soak the prunes in hot water for at least 2 hours, then drain. Transfer to a large heatproof bowl.

2 Boil the water in a saucepan and add the tea. Turn off the heat and leave to steep for 10 minutes. Strain and pour the tea over the prunes, then stir in the sugar and vanilla pod or extract. Leave the prunes to steep for 2–3 hours, then chill until ready to serve.

3 For the caramelized almonds, combine the almonds and sugar in a non-stick saucepan. Put over a high heat, stirring continuously, for 2–3 minutes. When the almonds start to brown, pour them into a heatproof dish. When they are completely cool, break them up. Set aside.

4 Serve the prunes cold, with a little of the tea mixture. Add a scoop of vanilla ice cream, if liked, and top with the caramelized almonds.

Sweet & Nutty
Caramel Strawberries

Makes 24

225g granulated sugar
3 tablespoons water
450g strawberries
3 tablespoons chopped, toasted
   hazelnuts

1 Put the sugar and water in a saucepan and heat gently until all the sugar has dissolved. Increase the heat and simmer for 6–10 minutes, or until golden. Take off the heat just before the caramel turns golden. If the caramel becomes too dark or smells burnt, plunge the base of the pan into a bowl of cold water to cool it down – being careful not to get any water into the caramel.

2 Take half the strawberries and, holding the strawberry by the stalk, dip the lower half of each one in the caramel. Set on a baking sheet lined with greaseproof paper and leave to harden. If the caramel in the pan hardens, return it to a very low heat and swirl it around until it softens.

3 Take the remaining strawberries, and dip the lower half in the caramel as before, then roll in the chopped nuts. Leave to harden.

Pineapple Upside-down Cake

Serves 8

55g butter
100g light brown sugar
425g can pineapple rings in natural
  juice, drained, reserving
  5 tablespoons juice
7 red glacé cherries
2 tablespoons whole pecan nuts
  (optional)
120g self-raising flour, sifted
1 teaspoon baking powder
Pinch of salt
225g caster sugar
3 eggs, separated
½ teaspoon vanilla extract
¼ teaspoon almond extract
Evaporated milk or single cream,
  to serve

1 Preheat the oven to 180°C/350°F/Gas mark 4. Reserve 1 tablespoon of the butter, then melt the rest in a saucepan over a low heat. Pour into a 23cm springform cake tin and sprinkle the light brown sugar evenly over it. Arrange the pineapple rings in the butter-sugar mixture, putting a cherry in the centre of each ring. Fill in the spaces with pecan nuts. Sift the flour, baking powder and salt together in another bowl. Cream the reserved 1 tablespoon of butter with the caster sugar in a separate bowl.

2 Beat the egg yolks in another bowl until pale, then slowly fold into the creamed mixture, continuing to beat until fluffy. Add the reserved pineapple juice, vanilla and almond extracts and the flour mixture. Whisk the egg whites in a clean, grease-free bowl until stiff peaks form, then fold into the mixture.

3 Pour the mixture over the pineapple. Bake for 30–35 minutes. Leave to cool in the tin on a wire rack. Loosen the cake with a palette knife, cover with a serving plate and invert, so that the pineapple and cherry base with its runny, butterscotch topping is now on top. Remove the tin. Serve warm with evaporated milk or single cream.

Summer Berry Galette

Serves 6

450g ready-made puff pastry
Plain flour, for dusting

For the filling
175g strawberries, hulled and sliced
115g raspberries
150g blueberries
25g icing sugar
40g ground almonds

1 Roll out the pastry on a lightly floured surface and cut a round 25cm in diameter. Put on a baking sheet and chill for 20 minutes.

2 Preheat the oven to 200°C/400°F/Gas mark 6. For the filling, mix all the fruit together and stir in the icing sugar. Sprinkle the ground almonds over the pastry and scatter the fruit on top, leaving a 1cm margin around the edge.

3 Bake in the oven for 20 minutes until the pastry is golden. Leave to stand for 1–2 minutes before serving.

Tip
Lightly grease or oil the baking sheet before placing the pastry round on it, otherwise it may stick.

Muscat-poached Grapes
with Thick Creamy Yoghurt

Serves 2

115g black seedless grapes
240ml Muscat dessert wine
2 tablespoons clear honey
1 vanilla pod, split lengthways
240ml Greek yoghurt

1 Put the grapes, wine, honey and vanilla pod in a saucepan and simmer for 5 minutes, or until the grapes have softened. Lift out the grapes using a slotted spoon and transfer them to a bowl.

2 Increase the heat and boil the syrup for 10 minutes, or until thick. Divide the yoghurt between 2 serving glasses and top with the grapes and their syrup.

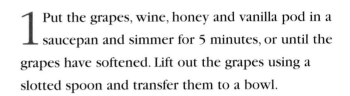

Tip
Use either grape juice, orange juice or apple juice in place of the Muscat wine, if you prefer.

Spiced Baked Apples

Serves 4

6 large dessert apples
75g unsalted butter, softened
50g light brown soft sugar
40g fresh white breadcrumbs
1 green cardamom pod
½ teaspoon ground cinnamon
¼ teaspoon freshly grated nutmeg
Pinch of saffron strands
Finely grated zest of ½ lemon
25g sultanas
25g shelled and chopped pistachio
   nuts
300ml dry cider
Single cream, to serve

1 Preheat the oven to 200°C/400°F/Gas mark 6. Core the apples leaving them whole. Using a small sharp knife, make a horizontal cut around the middle of the apples – this will prevent the skin from bursting during cooking.

2 Cream the butter, sugar and breadcrumbs together in a medium bowl. Using a pestle and mortar, crush the cardamom pod and remove the black seeds. Alternatively, use the back of a spoon.

3 Add the seeds to the butter mixture together with the cinnamon, nutmeg, saffron and lemon zest. Mix together well. Stir in the sultanas and pistachio nuts.

4 Divide this mixture among the 6 apples, stuffing it down tightly into where the cores used to be and piling any excess mixture on top of the apples. Transfer the apples to a ceramic or glass ovenproof dish large enough to hold them all with a little space in between. Pour the cider around the apples.

5 Transfer the dish to the oven and bake for about 40-45 minutes, or until the apples are very tender.

6 Serve warm with the juices from the baking dish and some cold cream.

Strawberries in Pimm's Syrup with Shortbread

Serves 2

120ml Pimm's
120ml orange juice
2 tablespoons caster sugar
2 fresh mint sprigs
200g strawberries, hulled and halved
4 shortbread cookies, to serve

1 Put the Pimm's, orange juice, sugar and mint in a mixing bowl. Add the strawberries and leave them to macerate at room temperature for 30 minutes.

2 Serve the strawberries and juices in small bowls with the shortbread cookies.

Tip
Try using mixed summer berries instead of the strawberries and serve with amaretti biscuits.

Orange Terrine
with Citrus Cream

Serves 4–6

5 large oranges
600ml fresh orange juice
50g caster sugar
6 sheets leaf gelatine
Sunflower oil, for oiling

For the citrus cream
2 tablespoons icing sugar
300ml whipping cream
1 tablespoon orange flower water
Grated zest and juice of 1 lemon
Grated zest of 1 lime

1 Cut the oranges into segments and put in a bowl. Put the orange juice and sugar in a saucepan and heat to nearly boiling. Remove from the heat.

2 Add the gelatine to the heated orange juice and stir until dissolved. Leave to cool.

3 Lightly oil a 1.2 litre capacity terrine mould and put a layer of orange segments across the base.

Continue to layer until three-quarters full. Pour the orange juice in and leave to set in the refrigerator for at least 6 hours. Turn out on to a flat serving plate.

4 For the citrus cream, just before serving sift the icing sugar into the cream, add the orange flower water and whip until soft peaks form. Stir in the lemon and lime zests, and the lemon juice. Serve with the terrine.

Tip
Top and tail the orange with a serrated fruit knife. Stand on one flat end and, following the curve of the orange, cut down the sides to remove the peel. Hold the orange in one hand and carefully cut down in between the membranes, releasing the segments which should now be clean and clear of any membranes.

Fresh Figs Baked

Serves 2

4 heaped tablespoons mascarpone
cheese
1 tablespoon Amaretto liqueur
4 plump figs, halved
2 tablespoons caster sugar
25g unsalted butter, softened
25g ground almonds
Pinch of freshly grated nutmeg

Tip
For an extra almond flavour, sprinkle a few toasted flaked almonds over the top before serving.

1 Mix the mascarpone and Amaretto liqueur together in a bowl until smooth. Set aside.

2 Preheat the grill. Put the figs cut-side up on a baking tray lined with greaseproof paper. Grill for 2 minutes, or until the flesh is softened.

3 Cream the sugar, butter, almonds and nutmeg together in a bowl. Put a spoonful on each fig half and grill for 1–2 minutes, keeping a careful eye on them, because they will burn quite quickly.

4 Serve the hot figs at once with a spoonful of the flavoured mascarpone.

Raspberry Surprise

Serves 4

3 egg whites
Pinch of salt
175g caster sugar
A drop of vanilla extract
300ml double cream
250g raspberries

1 Preheat the oven to 120°C/250°F/Gas mark ½. Line 2 baking sheets with non-stick baking paper. Set aside.

2 Using an electric whisk, beat the egg whites and salt together in a clean, grease-free bowl until stiff. Check this by lifting the whisk from the mixture and holding it upside down. If the tip of the egg white falls, the peak is soft. If it stands firm, it is stiff.

3 Add about half the sugar and whisk thoroughly. Keep whisking until the egg white no longer appears grainy and is shiny and smooth. Add more sugar, about 1 tablespoon at a time, whisking well between additions until all of it has been added. Add the vanilla. Keep whisking until smooth, thick and glossy. If the sugar is not whisked in well enough, it will melt and leach out during cooking.

4 Put 8 large spoonfuls of the mixture on to the prepared baking sheets, leaving plenty of space in between. Transfer to the oven and cook for 1 hour, switching the baking sheets over halfway through, then switch off the oven and leave until cold. This will give the meringues a crisp outside and chewy, 'marshmallowy' inside. If you prefer them crisper, cook for 1½ hours, then leave until cold.

5 Roughly crush the meringues and set aside. Whip the double cream in a large bowl until soft peaks form. Fold in the crushed meringues and raspberries. Serve immediately.

Tropical Fruit Salad

Serves 4

2.5cm piece fresh root ginger, peeled
425ml water
225g caster sugar
1 star anise
1 lemon grass stalk
2 kaffir lime leaves
1 mango
1 papaya
2 Nashi or other firm pears
1 melon, such as Ogen

1 Finely chop the ginger and put in a large saucepan with the water and sugar. Add the star anise, lemon grass and lime leaves. Bring to the boil, then simmer quite fiercely for 20 minutes until the water has reduced and the liquid is quite syrupy. Remove the lemon grass and lime leaves and leave to cool.

2 Peel and cut the mango into wedges and put into a mixing bowl.

3 Halve the papaya lengthways and scrape out the seeds. Peel carefully and cut into large wedges. Add to the mixing bowl.

4 Peel the pears and remove the core. Slice quite thickly and stir in with the other fruit.

5 Halve the melon and scrape out the seeds. Cut into quarters and remove the flesh from the rind. Cut into 1cm slices. Put in the mixing bowl. Pour the syrup over the fruit and serve chilled.

Blackcurrant Pudding

Serves 4

55g butter, at room temperature, plus
    extra for greasing
8 medium–thick slices of bread
225g fresh or frozen blackcurrants
5 eggs
75g granulated sugar
600ml whole milk, or single cream
2 teaspoons vanilla extract
Pinch of freshly grated nutmeg, plus
    extra for sprinkling
1 tablespoon demerara sugar,
    for sprinkling
Lightly whipped cream, to serve

1 Preheat the oven to 180°C/350°F/Gas mark 4. Grease a 1.2 litre baking dish.

2 Remove the crusts from the bread and discard. Spread the slices with the butter, then cut diagonally in half. Layer the bread slices in the dish, buttered-side up, scattering the blackcurrants between the layers as you go.

3 Whisk the eggs and sugar together lightly in a mixing bowl, then gradually whisk in the milk or cream, vanilla extract and nutmeg.

4 Pour the mixture over the bread, pushing the slices down well to soak them thoroughly. Sprinkle over the demerara sugar and some more nutmeg. Put the dish in a baking tin a quarter filled with hot water. Bake for 1 hour until the top is crisp and golden. Leave to cool slightly, then serve with lightly whipped cream.

Tarte Tatin

Serves 8

275g puff pastry, thawed if frozen
Plain flour, for dusting
Whipped cream or ice cream, to serve

For the filling
6 eating apples
1 tablespoon lemon juice
100g butter
6 tablespoons caster sugar

1 For the filling, peel, core and slice the apples into quarters, then use a fork to score the rounded side. Cut each quarter in half widthways, then toss the pieces in the lemon juice.

2 Melt the butter in a 23cm ovenproof frying pan. Stir in the sugar until it has melted, then remove the pan from the heat.

3 Arrange the apple quarters, scored-side down, in concentric circles in the pan. Pack them quite tightly. Put the pan over a low heat and cook, without disturbing the apples for 15 minutes, or until they begin to caramelize.

4 Put a baking sheet in the oven and preheat to 200°C/400°F/Gas mark 6. Roll out the puff pastry on a lightly floured surface to a round slightly larger than the top of the frying pan. Wrap it over the rolling pin, then place it on top of the apples in the pan. Tuck the edges inside the pan.

5 Transfer the frying pan to the oven and bake the tart for 20-25 minutes, or until the pastry is well risen and golden brown.

6 Leave the tart to cool for 5 minutes, then ease a knife between the top crust and the pan. Invert a plate on top then carefully turn both pan and plate over together so that the apples are on top. Serve warm, with whipped cream or ice cream.

Tip
Other types of fruit can be used to make similar tarts. Pears, plums, nectarines and apricots work well, as does rhubarb.

Berry Polenta Cake

Makes 8–10 slices

150g unsalted butter, softened, plus
   extra for greasing
150g caster sugar
100g ground almonds
80g instant polenta
4 eggs, beaten
Finely grated zest and juice of 1 large
   lemon
1 teaspoon baking powder
80g raspberries
80g blueberries
Golden caster sugar, for sprinkling

1 Preheat the oven to 180°C/350°F/Gas mark 4. Grease and base-line a 20cm round sandwich cake tin.

2 Beat the butter and sugar together in a bowl until creamy. Add the ground almonds, polenta, eggs, lemon zest and juice and baking powder and mix well. Add the raspberries and blueberries and stir in gently to mix.

3 Spoon the mixture into the prepared tin and level the surface. Bake in the oven for about 40 minutes, or until lightly browned and firm to the touch.

4 Remove the cake from the oven and leave to cool slightly in the tin, then turn out and put on a serving plate. Sprinkle with golden caster sugar and serve slightly warm or cold.

Seared Fruit in
Frothy Orange Sauce

Serves 4

2 fresh figs, cut into wedges

½ pineapple, peeled, cored and cut
  into chunks

1 ripe mango, peeled, stoned and cut
  into chunks

175g blackberries

4 tablespoons white wine

75g granulated sugar

6 egg yolks

2 tablespoons Cointreau or other
  orange liqueur

Tip
Keep a close eye on
the fruit while they are
cooking under the grill
as they are liable
to burn.

1 Divide the prepared fruit among 4 individual gratin dishes and scatter the blackberries over the top.

2 Heat the wine and sugar in a saucepan over a medium heat until the sugar has dissolved. Cook for 5 minutes.

3 Put the egg yolks in a large heatproof bowl. Set the bowl over a saucepan of simmering water and whisk the yolks until they have thickened and are pale and fluffy. Slowly pour the syrup into the egg yolks, with the Cointreau, whisking continuously until thickened.

4 Preheat the grill. Spoon the frothy mixture over the fruit and grill until the topping is golden. Serve immediately.

Gooseberry Pie

Serves 6

200g plain flour, plus extra for dusting
Pinch of salt
60g polenta
50g light brown sugar
140g butter, diced
3–4 tablespoons cold water
1 egg, beaten
Whipped cream or custard, to serve

For the filling
700g gooseberries
4 tablespoons caster sugar, plus extra
   for dusting

1 Sift the flour and salt into a mixing bowl. Add the polenta and sugar, then add the butter and rub it in until the mixture resembles fine breadcrumbs. Add 3 tablespoons cold water and mix to a firm dough, adding a little more water, if necessary. Knead briefly, then wrap in cling film and chill for 20 minutes.

2 For the filling, mix the gooseberries with the sugar. Divide the pastry into 2 pieces, one slightly larger than the other. Roll out the larger piece on a lightly floured surface and use to line a 20cm shallow pie dish. Spoon the gooseberries into the dish. Brush the rim of the pastry with a little beaten egg.

3 Roll out the remaining piece of pastry and lay it over the gooseberries. Press down and seal the edges. Cut off any overhanging pastry, crimp the edges and snip a steam hole in the top of the pie. Chill for 20 minutes.

4 Preheat the oven to 190°C/375°F/Gas mark 5. Brush the top of the pie with a little more egg and dust with sugar. Bake for 40 minutes, or until golden brown. Serve warm with whipped cream or custard.

Pavlova with Tropical Fruits

Serves 4–6

3 egg whites
Pinch of salt
175g caster sugar
A drop of vanilla extract
1 teaspoon cornflour
1 teaspoon wine vinegar
200ml double cream

For the filling
1 large mango, peeled and chopped
2 papayas, peeled and chopped
2 kiwi fruits, peeled and chopped
3 passion fruit

1 Preheat the oven to 120°C/250°F/Gas mark $\frac{1}{2}$. Line a baking sheet with non-stick baking paper. Set aside.

2 Using an electric whisk, beat the egg whites and salt together in a clean bowl until stiff. Check this by lifting the whisk from the mixture and holding it upside down. If the tip of the egg white falls, the peak is soft. If it stands firm, it is stiff.

3 Add about half the sugar and whisk well. Keep whisking until the egg white no longer appears grainy and is shiny and smooth. Add more sugar, about 1 tablespoon at a time, whisking thoroughly between additions until all of it has been added. Add the vanilla extract, cornflour and vinegar. Keep whisking until the mixture is smooth, thick and glossy.

4 Spread the meringue mixture on to the prepared baking sheet, in a 20cm diameter round, making a depression in the centre. Transfer to the oven and cook for 2 hours, then switch off the oven and leave until cold.

5 Whip the double cream until soft peaks form and use to fill the meringue shell. Put the fruit on top, then scoop the seeds from the passion fruit and drizzle over the top. Serve immediately.

- Chocolate Profiteroles
- Tarte au Citron
- Butterscotch Torte
- Devil's Food Cake with Chocolate Orange Icing
- Rhubarb & Custard Puff Pie
- Almond Pithiviers
- Champagne Jelly with Strawberries
- Passion Fruit Cheesecake
- Lemon Meringue Pie
- Burnt Custard
- Blueberry Streusel Tart
- Iced Summer Berries with Chocolate Sauce
- Chewy Meringues with Orange-scented Mascarpone
- Mango Sorbet
- Chocolate Truffles with Orange Flower Water

- Vanilla Poached Pears with Butterscotch Sauce
- Raspberry & Passionfruit Pavlova
- Summer Berry Tart
- Apple Pie
- Baked Peaches with Honey & Ricotta
- Crumble-topped Blackcurrant Pie with Cinnamon Pastry
- Spiced Palmiers with Apples & Raisins
- Persimmon & Passion Fruit Ice Cream
- Apple & Calvados Soufflé
- Baked Lemon Custards with Brandy Snaps
- Crème Brûlée with Lemon & Lime Shorties
- Crêpes Suzette
- Hazelnut Meringue Cake

CHAPTER SIX

DINNER PARTY DELIGHTS

Chocolate Profiteroles

Makes 12

120g plain flour
1 tablespoon icing sugar
About 200ml water
75g butter, diced
3 eggs, beaten
300ml double cream
2 tablespoons drinking chocolate
 powder

For the sauce
115g good-quality plain chocolate,
 broken into pieces
2 tablespoons golden syrup
25g butter
4 tablespoons water

1 Preheat the oven to 200°C/400°F/Gas mark 6. Sift the flour and icing sugar into a small bowl. Put the water and butter in a saucepan and heat gently until the butter has melted. Bring to the boil, then remove from the heat and quickly add the flour mixture, beating until smooth. Transfer to a bowl and leave to cool.

2 With a hand-held electric mixer, gradually beat the eggs into the mixture to make choux pastry. Fit a piping bag with a plain nozzle and fill with the paste. Pipe 12 rounds on to a non-stick baking sheet. Bake for 18–20 minutes until puffed and golden. Make a hole in the base of each profiterole and leave to cool on a wire rack.

3 Whip the cream with the chocolate powder until stiff. Fill a new piping bag with the chocolate cream and pipe carefully into the hole in the base of each individual profiterole.

4 For the sauce, put the chocolate, golden syrup, butter and water into a bowl and set over a saucepan of simmering water. Melt the chocolate and stir to mix. To serve, drizzle the warm chocolate sauce over the profiteroles.

Tarte au Citron

Serves 8

150g plain flour, plus extra for dusting
Pinch of salt
75g chilled butter
1 tablespoon caster sugar
1 egg yolk
1 tablespoon chilled water
Icing sugar, for dusting

For the filling
3 large lemons
5 eggs, lightly beaten
30g unsalted butter, melted
150g caster sugar

1 Sift the flour and salt into a mixing bowl. Add the butter and rub it in until the mixture resembles breadcrumbs. Stir in the sugar. Mix the egg yolk and water together, then sprinkle over the dry mixture and mix to a firm dough. Knead briefly, then wrap in cling film and chill for 1 hour.

2 Preheat the oven to 200°C/400°F/Gas mark 6. Roll the pastry out on a floured surface and use to line a 21cm round or 33 x 14cm rectangular loose-bottomed tart tin. Prick the base all over.

3 Line the pastry case with non-stick baking paper and fill with baking beans. Bake for 15 minutes. Remove the paper and beans, brush the inside of the case with 2 teaspoons of the beaten egg from the filling. Bake for 5 minutes. Reduce the temperature to 120°C/250°F/Gas mark $\frac{1}{2}$.

4 Grate the zest from the lemons. Squeeze the juice; you will need 180ml. Put the lemon zest and juice in a bowl with the eggs, butter and sugar. Beat until smooth.

5 Pour the filling into the pastry case and bake for 35–45 minutes, or until just set. Transfer the tin to a wire rack and leave for 10 minutes before removing the tart from the tin. Leave to cool, then chill. Dust with icing sugar before serving.

Butterscotch Torte

Serves 8

225g butter, at room temperature
225g caster sugar
4 eggs, beaten
2 teaspoons vanilla essence
200g self-raising flour, sifted

For the filling
120g butter
200g dark brown sugar
75ml boiling water
375ml double cream
250ml milk
3 tablespoons cornflour

1 Preheat the oven to 190°C/375°F/Gas mark 5. Butter and bottom-line three 18cm cake tins.

2 Beat the butter with the sugar until light and fluffy. Beat in the eggs, little by little, and fold in the vanilla essence and flour. Spoon into the cake pans and level off the top. Bake 20–25 minutes until firm, springy and golden. Turn out on to wire racks and let cool.

3 For the filling, melt the butter in a saucepan and stir in the sugar. Boil for 1 minute, then stir in the water – be careful, it will bubble up. Remove from the heat. Heat 125ml of the cream with the milk in a separate saucepan until it reaches boiling point.

4 In a large bowl, mix the cornflour with a little water. Add the hot cream and milk mixture and stir well. Whisk into the melted butter and sugar and cook for 1 minute over a low heat until thick. Set aside to cool completely.

5 Whip the remaining cream to soft peaks. Place one circle of sponge on a serving plate. Spread over a third of the butterscotch filling and cover with a third of the whipped cream. Press a second circle of sponge on top and repeat with the fillings.

6 Top with the final sponge circle and cover with the remaining butterscotch and cream. This cake will not keep for long and is best served on the day of baking.

Devil's Food Cake

with Chocolate Orange Icing

Makes 8–10 slices

150g unsalted butter, softened, plus
  extra for greasing
175g plain chocolate,
  broken into squares
100g caster sugar
6 large eggs, separated
75g plain flour
50g ground almonds

For the icing
200ml whipping cream
200g plain chocolate,
  broken into squares
2 teaspoons finely grated orange zest
Sugared orange slices, to decorate
Sifted icing sugar, for dusting (optional)

1 Preheat the oven to 180°C/350°F/Gas mark 4.
Grease and line a deep 20cm round cake tin.

2 For the cake, melt the chocolate in a heatproof
bowl set over a saucepan of simmering water.
Remove and cool slightly. Beat the butter and half of
the sugar together in a separate bowl until creamy.
Beat in the melted chocolate, then beat in the egg
yolks, one at a time.

3 Sift the flour and ground almonds into a
separate bowl. Whisk the egg whites in
a clean bowl until stiff, then gradually whisk
in the remaining sugar. Stir half of the whisked
egg whites into the chocolate mixture to loosen it
slightly, then fold in the flour mixture together with
the remaining whisked egg whites.

4 Spoon the mixture into the prepared tin
and level the surface. Bake in the oven for
50–60 minutes, or until a skewer inserted into
the centre comes out clean. Cool in the tin for
10 minutes, then turn out on to a wire rack and
leave to cool completely.

5 For the icing, heat the cream in a saucepan
until nearly boiling. Remove from the heat, stir
in the chocolate until melted, then stir in the
orange zest. Keep stirring until thick. Spread the
icing over the top and sides of the cake. Decorate
with sugared orange slices, then leave the icing to
set before dusting the cake with icing sugar.

Rhubarb & Custard Puff Pie

Serves 4–6

375g ready-made puff pastry
Plain flour, for dusting
1 egg, beaten
25g icing sugar, for dusting

For the filling
375g young rhubarb, cut into 5cm
  pieces
75g caster sugar
300ml ready-made custard
1 teaspoon vanilla extract

1 Preheat the oven to 180°C/350°F/Gas mark 4. For the filling, put the rhubarb in an ovenproof dish and sprinkle over the sugar. Cover and bake for 40 minutes, or until tender. Leave to cool.

2 Mix the custard and vanilla extract together in a bowl, then carefully stir in the rhubarb, being careful not to break the fruit.

3 Roll out the pastry on a lightly floured surface to form a 30 x 38cm rectangle and put on a non-stick baking sheet. Pile the custard and rhubarb mixture on to one half leaving a 2.5cm margin and brush with a little beaten egg.

4 Fold the pastry half over the filling and press down to seal the edges – crimp with your fingers or the back of a fork. Brush the top with a little more egg. Sift the sugar evenly over the top.

5 Bake the pie in the oven for 25–30 minutes until risen and golden. Leave to stand for 5 minutes before serving.

Almond Pithiviers

Serves 8

350g ready-made puff pastry,
    thawed if frozen
Plain flour, for dusting
1 egg, beaten
1 tablespoon icing sugar, for dusting

For the filling
240ml milk
1 teaspoon vanilla extract
3 egg yolks
150g caster sugar
1 heaped tablespoon cornflour
120g unsalted butter, softened
120g ground almonds

1 For the filling, put the milk and vanilla extract in a saucepan and slowly bring to the boil. Mix the egg yolks, 50g sugar and cornflour together in a bowl. Pour the vanilla-flavoured milk over the egg yolk mixture and stir.

2 Return the mixture to the pan and cook over a low heat, stirring for 1 minute, or until thick. Remove from the heat and leave to cool.

3 Beat the butter and 100g sugar together until light and fluffy. Stir in the ground almonds, then fold in the cold custard.

4 Divide the pastry into 2 pieces. Roll out one piece on a lightly floured surface to 3mm thick and cut out a 25cm round. Put on a non-stick baking sheet and spread the almond mixture over the pastry, leaving a 2.5cm margin around the edge. Brush the edge with beaten egg.

5 Roll out the remaining pastry to the same thickness and cut a 28cm round. Lay it over the almond-topped pastry and press down to seal the edges. Chill for 30 minutes.

6 Preheat the oven to 200°C/400°F/Gas mark 6. Brush the surface with beaten egg and score the top in a diamond pattern. Bake for 35–40 minutes until golden. Leave to stand for 5 minutes before dusting with icing sugar and serving.

Tip
This dessert is best eaten on the day it is made. Serve with some good-quality vanilla ice cream, if liked.

Champagne Jelly
with Strawberries

Serves 2

120g caster sugar
180ml water
180ml champagne
3 sheets gelatine, soaked in
    4 tablespoons water
Strawberries and single cream,
    to serve

1 Put the sugar and water in a small saucepan over a low heat and stir until dissolved. Increase the heat and boil for about 5 minutes, or until syrupy.

2 Take the pan off the heat and add just enough of the champagne to cool the syrup slightly. Beat in the soaked gelatine, until it has completely dissolved, then pour in the remaining champagne.

3 Pour the mixture into two 180ml moulds or one 350ml mould, and put in the refrigerator to set. Unmould by inverting on to a plate and giving the mould a short, sharp shake. Serve with fresh strawberries and cream.

Tip
Before adding the champagne and gelatine in step 2 make sure the syrup is hot enough to melt the gelatine but cool enough not to cook it, otherwise the jelly will not set properly.

Passion Fruit Cheesecake

Serves 8–10

150g digestive biscuits
90g butter, melted
9 passion fruits, halved
750g cream cheese
120g caster sugar
125ml single cream
4 eggs, beaten
3 egg yolks
2 teaspoons vanilla extract

1 Put the biscuits in a food processor and process until they are broken into crumbs. Add the melted butter and process to mix. Press the mixture into the base of a 23cm springform cake tin and chill for 20 minutes until firm. Cover the outside of the tin with a layer of aluminium foil.

2 Preheat the oven to 160°C/325°F/Gas mark 3. Put a sieve over a bowl and spoon in the pulp from 6 of the passion fruits. With the back of a wooden spoon extract as much juice from the seeds as possible.

3 Put the cream cheese, sugar and cream in a food processor and process until smooth. Pour in the eggs and egg yolks and process again until well mixed. Add the vanilla extract and passion fruit juice and process briefly. Pour the cheesecake mixture into the tin.

4 Put the tin in a shallow dish and pour in enough water to come quarter-way up the sides of the tin. Bake for 1½ hours until just firm. (The aluminium foil around the tin will stop the water from leaking into the cheesecake.) Turn off the oven and leave the cheesecake in the oven for an extra 10 minutes.

5 Chill the cheesecake for at least 3–4 hours. Once firm, remove the sides of the tin. Spoon the pulp from the remaining passion fruits over the cheesecake just before serving.

Lemon Meringue Pie

Serves 8

23cm baked pastry case

For the filling
225g granulated sugar
25g cornflour
250ml boiling water
3 egg yolks, lightly beaten
25g butter
Finely grated zest and juice of
   2 large lemons

For the meringue
3 egg whites, at room temperature
¼ teaspoon cream of tartar
6 tablespoons granulated sugar
½ teaspoon vanilla extract

1 Preheat the oven to 230°C/450°F/Gas mark 8. For the filling, combine the sugar and cornflour over a low heat and slowly add the boiling water, stirring continuously. Bring to the boil, then simmer still stirring for about 5 minutes until the mixture becomes transparent and thickens.

2 Put the lightly beaten egg yolks in a separate bowl. Remove the sugar and cornflour mixture from the heat and gradually pour the hot liquid into the yolks. Set the bowl over a saucepan of simmering water. Stir in the butter, lemon juice and zest and continue to cook until the filling becomes very thick. Leave to cool, then pour into the pastry case.

3 For the meringue, whisk the egg whites in a clean bowl until frothy. Add the cream of tartar and continue whisking. Drizzle in the sugar and vanilla extract and continue whisking until stiff peaks form. Take care not to overwhisk.

4 Pile the meringue on to the lemon filling, swirling lightly from the centre towards the edges, ensuring that it touches the pastry all around. Use the tip of a knife to gently pull the meringue into peaks. Bake in the centre of the oven for about 10-15 minutes until the meringue is a delicate brown. Serve warm.

Burnt Custard

Serves 4

400ml double cream
1 vanilla pod, split in half
5 egg yolks
100g granulated sugar
4 tablespoons bourbon

Tip

If using a blow torch to caramelise the top, make sure you use a culinary blow torch available from kitchenware shops.

1 Preheat the oven to 200°C/400°F/Gas mark 6. Heat the cream and vanilla pod in a saucepan over a low heat until almost boiling, then leave to infuse for 10 minutes. Whisk the egg yolks with 5 tablespoons sugar in a bowl until pale and thickened slightly. Stir in the hot vanilla cream and bourbon.

2 Pour into four 150ml ramekins and put them in a roasting tin. Pour in warm water to come halfway up the sides. Bake for 12–15 minutes until a skin has formed, but the custard is still wobbly.

3 Chill the ramekins at least 3 hours. Preheat the grill. Scatter the remaining sugar over the tops. Cook under the hot grill or use a blow torch to caramelise the sugar. Leave the caramel to cool before serving.

Blueberry Streusel Tart

Serves 8

125g butter, softened, plus extra for
   greasing
3 tablespoons caster sugar
1 egg
300g plain flour
60ml single cream
½ teaspoon vanilla extract
2 tablespoons finely ground almonds
2 tablespoons soft white breadcrumbs
Natural yoghurt, to serve

For the filling
700g blueberries
100g caster sugar
5 tablespoons soft white breadcrumbs
3 tablespoons flaked almonds
2 tablespoons light brown sugar
½ teaspoon ground cinnamon

1 Put a baking sheet in the oven and preheat to 200°C/400°F/Gas mark 6. Grease a 27cm tart tin. Beat the butter and sugar together in a bowl. When the mixture is light and fluffy, beat in the egg with a little of the flour.

2 Stir in the remaining flour alternately with the cream and vanilla extract, mixing to a smooth, soft dough. Spoon the dough into the tin, then gently ease it evenly over the base of the tin and up the sides.

3 Mix the ground almonds and breadcrumbs together, and sprinkle the mixture evenly over the base of the pastry case.

4 For the filling, mix the blueberries with the sugar and half the breadcrumbs. Spoon the mixture into the pastry case.

5 Mix the remaining breadcrumbs, flaked almonds, brown sugar and cinnamon together in another bowl. Scatter the mixture evenly over the blueberries.

6 Bake for 30 minutes, or until the pastry is cooked and the streusel topping is golden. Serve warm with yoghurt.

Iced Summer Berries

with Chocolate Sauce

Serves 4

350g mixed summer berries, such as
   strawberries, blueberries, raspberries
   or blackberries
250ml double cream
1 teaspoon vanilla extract
75g white chocolate,
   broken into pieces

1 Put the berries in a large flat dish and freeze for 45 minutes.

2 Heat the cream and vanilla extract in a saucepan until it reaches boiling point. Add the chocolate and stir until melted and the sauce is smooth. Pour into a jug and serve warm with the iced berries.

Tip
For a dark sauce, replace the white chocolate with the same quantity of milk chocolate.

Chewy Meringues
with Orange-scented Mascarpone

Makes 2

3 egg whites
150g caster sugar
½ teaspoon white wine vinegar
1 heaped teaspoon cornflour

For the topping
100g mascarpone cheese
3 tablespoons orange juice
Zest of 1 orange
½ pomegranate

1 Preheat the oven to 140°C/275°F/Gas mark 1. Put the egg whites in a clean, grease-free bowl and beat until stiff. Add 75g of the sugar, a tablespoonful at a time, beating after each addition until glossy. Add the remaining sugar and beat gently. Mix the vinegar and cornflour together in a small bowl and stir into the mixture.

2 Spoon the mixture on to greaseproof paper to make two 10cm rounds. Bake for 1 hour, then leave to cool.

3 Meanwhile, mix the mascarpone, orange juice and zest together. Bash the back of the pomegranate with a rolling pin to remove the seeds. Top the meringues with the mascarpone mixture and scatter the pomegranate seeds on top. Serve immediately.

Mango Sorbet

Serves 8

475ml water
450g caster sugar
1 vanilla pod, split lengthways
450g mango, fresh, canned
  or frozen, peeled and chopped
Juice of 1 lime
2 tablespoons stem ginger, chopped
Fresh mint sprigs, to decorate
Dessert biscuits, to serve

1 Pour the water into a saucepan and add the sugar and vanilla pod. Bring to the boil and simmer for 2 minutes.

2 Remove the pan from the heat and leave to cool completely. When ready to use, remove the vanilla pod, split it in half and scrape down the inside to remove the seeds. Put the seeds into the syrup and discard the pod.

3 Put the mango in a blender and purée, or mash well by hand. Add the lime juice and vanilla syrup and mix well.

4 If using an ice cream maker, follow the manufacturer's instructions to make a sorbet. If making by hand, pour the mixture into a freezerproof container and freeze for 4 hours. Beat in a food processor until smooth, then return to the container and freeze again.

5 When firm, scoop the sorbet into bowls and top with stem ginger. Decorate with a mint sprig, and serve with dessert biscuits.

Chocolate Truffles
with Orange Flower Water

Makes 10

80ml double cream
150g white chocolate
1–2 tablespoons orange flower water
4 tablespoons cocoa powder

Tip
For dark chocolate truffles, replace the white chocolate with plain and use brandy instead of the orange flower water.

1 Heat the cream in a small saucepan until almost boiling. Take off the heat, leave to cool for 5 minutes, or until warm enough to touch, then stir in the chocolate and orange flower water until smooth.

2 Dust your hands in a little cocoa and put the remainder on a flat plate. Scoop out a walnut-sized piece of chocolate with a spoon and roll it in your hands. Roll in cocoa and put on a clean plate. Repeat with the remaining mixture. Chill for 1 hour to firm up before serving.

Vanilla Poached Pears

with Butterscotch Sauce

Serves 6

6 ripe pears, peeled
750ml–1 litre water
175g caster sugar
2 vanilla pods, split lengthways
Pared zest of ½ lemon
Vanilla ice cream or whipped cream, to
    serve (optional)

For the sauce
55g butter
75g light brown sugar
125ml golden syrup
125ml double cream

1 Stand the pears in a saucepan just big enough for them to fit snugly. Pour enough water over to just cover and add the sugar, vanilla pods and lemon zest.

2 Bring to the boil, then reduce the heat and simmer for 40-50 minutes until the pears are softened but still hold their shape. (If the pears aren't very ripe this might take a bit longer.) Remove from the heat and leave the pears to cool in the syrup.

3 For the butterscotch sauce, melt the butter with the light brown sugar and golden syrup. Stir in 125ml of the cooled pear syrup and simmer for 2-3 minutes. Stir in the cream and simmer for a further 2-3 minutes.

4 Remove the pears to a serving dish and either pour a little butterscotch sauce over each pear, or serve it separately in a jug. Serve with vanilla ice cream or whipped cream.

Raspberry & Passion Fruit
Pavlova

Serves 4–6

4 egg whites
225g caster sugar
1 teaspoon white wine vinegar
1½ teaspoons cornflour
1 teaspoon vanilla extract

For the topping
600ml double cream
350g fresh raspberries
4 passion fruit
Fresh mint sprigs
Icing sugar for dusting

1 Preheat the oven to 180°C/350°F/Gas mark 4. Line a baking tray with baking paper. Whisk the egg whites in a clean bowl until stiff. Whisk in the sugar 1 tablespoon at a time, whisking between each addition.

2 Blend the vinegar, cornflour and vanilla extract together in a small bowl, then whisk into the meringue mixture.

3 Spoon the mixture on to the paper-lined baking tray and spread out to a 25cm round. Make a slight dip in the centre. Bake for 5 minutes. Reduce the oven temperature to 150°C/300°F/Gas mark 2, then bake for 1¼ hours, or until firm to the touch and lightly golden. Turn off the oven and leave to cool in the oven for 2–3 hours.

4 Slide a palette knife under the pavlova and transfer to a flat serving plate. Whip the cream until soft peaks form and spoon into the centre of the pavlova.

5 Scatter the raspberries over the top. Scoop the seeds and pulp out of the passion fruit and scatter on to the raspberries. Decorate with mint sprigs and dust with icing sugar.

Summer Berry Tart

Serves 6–8

275g plain flour, plus extra for dusting
25g icing sugar
175g unsalted butter
2 egg yolks
4 tablespoons cold water
Icing sugar, for dusting

For the filling
600ml milk
4 egg yolks
75g caster sugar
25g plain flour
25g cornflour
Grated zest of 1 orange
150ml double cream
450g mixed summer berries, such as
   raspberries, strawberries, blueberries
   and redcurrants

1 Sift the flour and icing sugar into a mixing bowl. Add the butter and rub it in until the mixture resembles breadcrumbs. Whisk the egg yolks with the cold water. Make a well in the centre of the flour, add the egg mixture and mix to a firm dough. Knead briefly, then wrap in cling film and chill for 20 minutes.

2 Roll out the pastry on a lightly floured surface and use to line a 24-cm loose-bottomed tart tin. Prick the base and chill for 10 minutes.

3 Preheat the oven to 190°C/375°F/Gas mark 5. Line the pastry case with non-stick baking paper and fill with baking beans. Bake for 20 minutes until golden and crisp. Remove the paper and beans and leave to cool on a wire rack.

4 For the filling, pour the milk into a non-stick saucepan and bring to the boil. Mix the egg yolks with the sugar, and stir in the flour and cornflour. Pour the mixture into the hot milk and mix well.

5 Bring the milk mixture to the boil, stirring continuously to prevent lumps forming. Once the custard is thick and smooth, remove from the heat and stir in the orange zest. Cover and chill.

6 Whip the cream in a bowl until soft peaks form, then fold into the cold custard. Spoon the custard into the pastry case and level off. Arrange the mixed summer fruit over the custard and dust with icing sugar before serving.

Apple Pie

Serves 8

450g plain flour, plus extra for dusting
½ teaspoon salt
115g butter
100g white vegetable fat
Iced water
Milk, for glazing
Caster sugar, for dusting

For the filling

900g cooking apples, peeled, cored
  and thinly sliced
2 teaspoons lemon juice
6 tablespoons raisins
1 teaspoon pared orange zest
225g light brown sugar
4 teaspoons cornflour
1 teaspoon ground cinnamon
1 teaspoon freshly grated nutmeg
4 teaspoons butter

1 Sift the flour and salt into a mixing bowl. Add the butter and vegetable fat and rub them in until the mixture resembles breadcrumbs. Add just enough iced water and mix to a firm dough. Knead briefly, then wrap in cling film and leave to chill for 30 minutes.

2 Put a baking sheet in the oven and preheat to 200°C/400°F/Gas mark 6. For the filling, put the sliced apples into a bowl. Toss with the lemon juice, then add all the remaining filling ingredients, except the butter, and mix lightly.

3 Roll out just less than half the pastry on a lightly floured surface and use to line a 25cm pie dish. Add the filling, mounding it into the centre, then dot with the butter.

4 Roll out the remaining pastry and make a lid for the pie. Seal and crimp the edges and snip 2 steam vents. Brush the surface lightly with milk and sprinkle with sugar. Bake for 15 minutes, then reduce the oven temperature to 180°C/350°F/Gas mark 4 and bake for a further 20 minutes. Serve hot or cold.

Baked Peaches
with Honey & Ricotta

Serves 2

2 ripe peaches
4 tablespoons ricotta cheese
2 tablespoons Amaretto liqueur
2 tablespoons clear honey
Redcurrant sprigs, to decorate
   (optional)

1 Preheat the oven to 200°C/400°F/Gas mark 6. Halve the peaches and carefully lever out the stones using the point of a knife. Put the peaches cut-side up in a small roasting tin and put a tablespoon of ricotta cheese in the centre of each half.

2 Mix the Amaretto and honey together in a small bowl, then drizzle the mixture over the peaches and ricotta.

3 Bake for 10–15 minutes, then spoon into bowls and drizzle over any juices from the roasting tin. Serve hot, topped with sprigs of redcurrants.

Tip
Advance preparation:
The topping will keep in a covered container in the refrigerator for up to 2 days. Bake the fruit, cover, and refrigerate the day of serving. Assemble the dessert just before serving.

Crumble-topped
Blackcurrant Pie with Cinnamon Pastry

Serves 6–8

225g plain flour, plus extra for dusting
Pinch of salt
1 teaspoon ground cinnamon
120g unsalted butter, diced
3–4 tablespoons cold water
Whipped cream, to serve

For the filling
675g blackcurrants
75g caster sugar

For the crumble topping
175g plain flour
Pinch of salt
120g butter, diced
70g light soft brown sugar
75g flaked almonds

1 Sift the flour, salt and cinnamon into a mixing bowl. Add the butter and rub it in until the mixture resembles breadcrumbs. Add just enough water and mix to a firm dough. Knead briefly, then wrap and chill for 30 minutes.

2 Roll out the dough on a lightly floured surface to line a 23-cm loose-bottomed tart tin. Prick the pastry and chill for 10 minutes.

3 Preheat the oven to 200°C/400°F/Gas mark 6. Line the pastry case with non-stick baking paper and fill with baking beans. Bake for about 20 minutes. Remove the paper and beans and bake for 10 minutes until pale golden. Leave to cool.

4 Mix the blackcurrants and sugar together in a bowl and set aside.

5 For the crumble topping, put the flour and salt into a large bowl. Add the butter and rub it in until coarsely combined, with largish lumps of butter still showing. Stir in the brown sugar.

6 Spoon the blackcurrants into the pastry case and top evenly with the crumb mixture. Sprinkle over the flaked almonds. Bake for 20–25 minutes until golden and bubbling. Serve warm with whipped cream.

Spiced Palmiers
with Apples & Raisins

Makes about 36 biscuits

For the palmiers
450g ready-made puff pastry
Plain flour, for dusting
4 tablespoons caster sugar
2 tablespoons icing sugar
1 teaspoon ground cinnamon
½ teaspoon ground ginger
½ teaspoon freshly grated nutmeg
150ml whipped cream, to serve

For the apple and raisin compote
450g Bramley apples, roughly chopped
4 tablespoons granulated sugar
1 tablespoon raisins
1 tablespoon cranberries
2 teaspoons grated orange zest

1 Roll the puff pastry out thinly on a lightly floured surface and trim to a 25 x 40cm rectangle. Cut the pastry in two to make two smaller rectangles. Sift the caster sugar, icing sugar and spices together. Dust both sides of both pastry sheets with about a quarter of the spiced sugar.

2 Working one rectangle at a time, lay the pastry in front of you with one long edge nearest you. Fold the pastry in half, away from you, then unfold to give a crease down the middle. Fold the edge of the pastry nearest you halfway to the crease and repeat with the edge of the pastry furthest from you. Dust liberally with the spiced sugar.

3 Repeat the fold so the edge nearest you meets the edge furthest from you in the middle where you creased the pastry originally. Dust with sugar and reserve any leftover. Fold again down the crease to give a long thin rectangle. This will give you 6 layers. Repeat with the second rectangle. Wrap each in clingfilm and freeze for 1 hour.

4 Preheat the oven to 180°C/350°F/Gas mark 4. Dust the pastry with any remaining sugar. Cut each crossways into 18 slices. Lay the slices on a baking sheet and bake for 10 minutes, then turn and bake for 5–10 minutes until golden. Cool.

5 Put all the compote ingredients in a saucepan. Cover and cook over a low heat for 15 minutes. Stir and cool. Serve the palmiers with the compote and whipped cream.

Persimmon & Passion Fruit
Ice Cream

Serves 4

3 ripe persimmons
3 passion fruits, halved
Juice of 1 lemon
5 tablespoons caster sugar
300ml double cream
Extra passion fruit pulp, to serve

1 Cut the top off each persimmon and spoon the persimmon flesh into a bowl, using a teaspoon to scrape as much flesh off the skins as possible. Put a sieve over the bowl. Scrape the passion fruit pulp into the sieve, then press it through with the back of a spoon, leaving the black seeds behind.

2 Spoon the mixture into a food processor, add the lemon juice and sugar and process to a fine purée. With the motor running, gradually add the cream until well combined.

3 Pour into a freezerproof container and freeze for about 2–3 hours, or until half-frozen, then beat to break up any ice crystals. Repeat this process twice more until the ice cream holds its shape. Alternatively, churn in an ice cream maker.

4 Before serving, let the ice cream soften for 20–30 minutes. Serve in scoops with a little passion fruit pulp spooned over the top.

Apple & Calvados Soufflé

Serves 6

45g butter, plus extra
   for greasing
1 tablespoon digestive biscuit crumbs
40g plain flour
185ml milk
3 tablespoons Calvados or other
   apple brandy
2 tart dessert apples, peeled,
   cored and sliced
2 teaspoons grated lemon zest
2 tablespoons fresh lemon juice
120g caster sugar
4 eggs, separated
Icing sugar, for dusting

1 Preheat the oven to 190°C/375°F/Gas mark 5. Grease six 300ml soufflé dishes or a 1.75 litre soufflé dish and scatter the biscuit crumbs around the sides and over the base.

2 Melt the remaining butter in a saucepan and add the flour. Remove from the heat and gradually stir in the milk. Return the pan to the heat and bring to the boil, whisking gently until the mixture thickens. Cook for 1 minute, then remove from the heat and whisk in the Calvados. Cover the sauce and set aside to cool.

3 Cook the apples with the lemon zest and juice and 1 tablespoon of the caster sugar in a covered saucepan, stirring occasionally, for 5-6 minutes until softened. Transfer to a blender or food processor and process until puréed, then leave to cool slightly. Meanwhile, whisk the egg yolks into the cooled sauce, then stir in the apple purée.

4 Whisk the egg whites in a clean, grease-free bowl until stiff. Gradually whisk in the remaining sugar until the mixture is glossy. Stir a spoonful of the whites into the sauce, then fold in the rest. Spoon the mixture into the individual soufflé dishes or large soufflé dish. Wipe the top of the dishes and bake for 20-35 minutes, depending on the size of the dish. Resist the temptation to open the oven door while cooking. Dust the top with icing sugar before serving.

Baked Lemon Custards

with Brandy Snaps

Serves 6

600ml double cream
8 egg yolks
175g icing sugar, sifted
Juice of 4 lemons

For the brandy snaps
120g butter, plus extra for greasing
120g granulated sugar
4 tablespoons golden syrup
120g plain flour
Juice of 1 lemon
Pinch of ground ginger

1 Preheat the oven to 150°C/300°F/Gas mark 2. Mix the double cream, egg yolks, icing sugar and lemon juice together in a bowl and pour into 6 ramekins. Half-fill a roasting tin with hot water and put the ramekins in the tin. Bake for 1 hour. Remove and leave to chill for 4 hours.

2 Preheat the oven to 190°C/375°F/Gas mark 5. For the brandy snaps, grease a large baking sheet and the handles of 6 wooden spoons or something of a similar size.

3 Melt the butter, sugar and golden syrup in a saucepan. Remove from the heat and stir in the flour, lemon juice and ground ginger.

4 Put teaspoons of the mixture on the baking sheet, making sure you leave a gap of at least 15cm as the mixture spreads during cooking. Bake for 5–6 minutes until golden brown. Set aside the brandy snaps for a few minutes until cool enough to handle. Shape each one around the handle of a wooden spoon. When cold and crisp, slip the brandy snaps off the handles and store in an airtight container until ready to serve with the custards.

Crème Brûlée

with Lemon & Lime Shorties

Serves 6

600ml double cream
1 vanilla pod, split
6 egg yolks
3 tablespoons granulated sugar
175g icing sugar, sifted

For the shorties
120g plain flour, plus extra for dusting
55g cornflour
55g granulated sugar
Grated zest of 1 lemon and 1 lime
120g unsalted butter

1 Preheat the oven to 150°C/300°F/Gas mark 2. Heat the cream with the vanilla pod until it reaches boiling point. Whisk the egg yolks and granulated sugar together in a bowl, then pour the mixture over the hot cream.

2 Stir the mixture over a low heat until it thickens enough to coat the back of a wooden spoon. Strain into a jug, then pour into 6 ramekins.

3 Stand the ramekins in a roasting tin half-full of water and bake for 1 hour. Leave to cool, then chill for at least 3 hours. Just before serving, preheat the grill. Dust thickly with the icing sugar. Put the ramekins under the hot grill for 3–4 minutes until the sugar caramelises. Leave to chill for 30 minutes.

4 Make the shorties while the crèmes brûlées are baking. Preheat the oven to 160°C/325°F/Gas mark 3. Mix the flour, cornflour, sugar and lemon and lime zests together in a bowl. Add the butter and rub it in until the mixture resembles breadcrumbs. Bring the crumbs together to form a smooth ball. Roll the dough out onto a lightly floured surface and stamp out 12–14 rounds with a 7.5cm biscuit cutter.

5 Put on a non-stick baking sheet and bake for 20 minutes, or until golden brown. Leave to cool until crisp, then store in an airtight container until ready to serve.

Crêpes Suzette

Makes eight 20cm pancakes

115g plain flour
Pinch of salt
2 medium eggs, beaten
300ml milk
Zest of 1 orange
1 tablespoon caster sugar
Vegetable oil, for frying

To serve
Zest of 1 orange
Zest of 1 lemon
1 tablespoon caster sugar
150ml orange juice
50g unsalted butter
3 tablespoons Cointreau

1 Sift the flour and salt into a mixing bowl. Add the eggs and half the milk. Whisk until thick and smooth. Gradually whisk in the remaining milk until you have a smooth batter the consistency of single cream. Add the orange zest and sugar and mix. Cover and leave to stand for 20–30 minutes.

2 Lightly oil a 20cm crêpe pan or frying pan. Put the pan over a medium heat. Pour in about 2 tablespoons of the batter and swirl the pan to coat the base thinly and evenly. Cook for about 1 minute until the edges appear dry, then carefully flip or turn the pancake, allowing it to cook on the other side for about 30 seconds. Repeat with remaining batter, stacking pancakes between sheets of kitchen paper as you go and keeping them warm until ready to serve.

3 To serve, mix the citrus zest, sugar and orange juice together. Heat a large frying pan and add the butter. When melted and foaming, add the juice mixture and bring to the boil for 1–2 minutes until slightly thickened. Fold the pancakes into triangles and add to the pan to heat through. Pour over the liqueur and set alight. Serve once the flames have subsided.

Tip
You can use any other orange liqueur, if you like. These pancakes are wonderful served with pouring cream.

Hazelnut Meringue Cake

Serves 6–8

Butter, for greasing
4 egg whites
200g caster sugar
1 teaspoon vanilla extract
1 teaspoon cider vinegar
1 teaspoon cornflour
80g toasted hazelnuts, finely ground
2 tablespoons coarsely chopped
   toasted hazelnuts

For the filling
75g natural yoghurt
2 tablespoons whisky
2 tablespoons clear honey
125ml double or whipping cream
225g fresh raspberries
Icing sugar, for dusting

1 Preheat the oven to 180°C/350°F/Gas mark 4. Grease and base-line two 20cm round sandwich cake tins.

2 For the meringue, whisk the egg whites in a clean bowl until stiff peaks form. Gradually whisk in the sugar to make a stiff and glossy meringue. Fold in the vanilla extract, vinegar, cornflour and ground hazelnuts.

3 Divide the mixture evenly between the two prepared tins and level the surface. Scatter the chopped hazelnuts over the top of one, then bake in the oven for 50–60 minutes, or until crisp. Turn out on to a wire rack and leave to cool.

4 For the filling, stir the yoghurt, whisky and honey together in a bowl. Whip the cream in a separate bowl until soft peaks form, then fold into the yoghurt mixture together with the raspberries.

5 Sandwich the two meringues together with the cream mixture, with the nut-topped meringue uppermost. Dust with icing sugar and serve in slices.

Index